How to Pass
English for Business

FIRST LEVEL
(Third edition)

How to Pass
English for Business

LCCI
EXAMINATIONS
BOARD

FIRST LEVEL
(Third edition)

Allan Sharples
BA (Hons) PGCE DipME

London Chamber of Commerce and Industry Examinations Board
Athena House
112 Station Road
Sidcup
Kent DA15 7BJ
United Kingdom

First published in Germany by Logophon Lehrmittel Verlag 1994
Reprinted 1997
New (third) edition published in Great Britain by the London Chamber of
Commerce and Industry Examinations Board 2001

Reprinted 2001

New (third) edition © LCCI CET 2001

British Library Cataloguing-in-Publication Data
Sharples, Allan
    How to pass English for Business, First Level. – 3rd ed.
    1. English language – Business English – Examinations –
    Study guides 2. English language – Textbooks for foreign
    speakers
    I. Title
    428'.002465

ISBN 1 86247 003 0

**This is the only book endorsed by LCCIEB for use by students
of this LCCIEB examination subject at this level. No other book is
endorsed by LCCIEB for this subject at this level.**

10   9   8   7   6   5   4   3   2

Typeset by ↗\ Tek-Art, Croydon, Surrey
Printed in The United Kingdom by Astron Limited, Huntingdon, Cambridgeshire

Contents

Contents

Figures

About the author

Allan Sharples is the Chief Examiner of English for Business First Level with the LCCIEB.

Allan originally took his degree in English, French and Drama at Bristol University in 1962. He followed this with post-graduate work in the USA and a PGCE course at the London Institute of Education. In 1985 he completed a Diploma in Educational Management at the University of Manchester.

Allan has taught for 30 years and was a secondary headteacher from 1985–95. He has conducted teacher training programmes in English for Business for LCCIEB in China, Vietnam and Jugoslavia.

The Candidate's Book and the Teacher's Guide

This new edition of the Candidate's Book for *How to Pass English for Business First Level* links with the Teacher's Guide. The sections and chapters follow the same sequence. The exercises are similar in the way they build the necessary skills for success. All the source material is, however, completely new and different from that in the Teacher's Guide.

The Candidate's Book has added features to suit the student working alone, and contains within the text full advice on techniques and methodology of preparation for the English for Business First Level examination.

The books can be used in conjunction with one another to provide a wealth of advice and practical material for use by a single person or a group situation.

Note on English for Business examinations

On 1 January 1999, LCCIEB's English for Business (EFB) examinations were aligned with the new LCCIEB Language Levels framework. In addition to specifying precisely which 'business language' content each examination should contain, the LCCIEB Levels also comply with the following 2 important official frameworks: the Council of Europe's Language Levels, and the British National Standards (NVQ) for languages.

In the case of English for Business First Level, the corresponding official levels are the Council of Europe's Waystage Level, and the British National Standards (NVQ) Level 1.

Note on product names

This book includes some names that are or are claimed to be owned by certain commercial organisations. For legal purposes, the inclusion of these words does not suggest that they are no longer owned by a specific company or that they have passed into general use, nor is any other understanding implied regarding their legal status. Every effort has been made by the Publisher to seek the permission of the owners to include their product names in this book. The Publisher will rectify any credit omissions or errors in a subsequent edition of this book, should notification of any such error be made at any time.

Part 1
English for Business
First Level

1

General information

1.1 Introduction

Students starting new courses are eager for success in their chosen field of study. More often than not, particularly if the course subject is a new one, the student will hope that this success will lead to further successes in the field. It may also be a stepping stone to a new job. Students, therefore, want to make sure that the effort and commitment they are giving to their studies will not be wasted. Time is a precious commodity, and we all need to feel that we are spending it wisely and to good effect. 'No time-wasting, please' is the golden rule.

This book will, we hope, prevent time-wasting in preparing you for the English for Business First Level examination. It is written by a teacher and a Chief Examiner with over 30 years' experience in helping students reach their goals. The guidelines, practice exercises and answer keys will train you to complete the course successfully and enjoyably. The full syllabus is covered in detail.

For your part, as a student, you will be expected:

- to show commitment
- to follow instructions precisely
- not to take short-cuts
- above all, to do all that you are asked before looking at the answer keys.

If you are also following a college course in EFB 1, this book will act as a complementary guide. If you are working on your own (or better still, with a friend) it provides everything that you need for success.

It is important to state that this is not a course in business expertise. It will not tell you how to take over Microsoft or the Bank of England! It is about thinking and responding to situations in a business context, and about developing the skills and understanding in basic communication to deal with those same situations, whether it is a letter, a memo, or the simple analysis of given data.

English for Business First Level is an internationally recognised qualification in its own right, and also a stepping stone to the higher levels of English for Business provided by the London Chamber of Commerce and Industry Examinations Board (LCCIEB). Business expertise is not required at First Level. The course focuses on communication and reading skills centred upon simple office situations. Every examination question provides the necessary information and background material. Students who develop the skills of:

- careful reading and understanding of the text
- selecting relevant information
- writing straightforward letters and memos

will have no difficulty in obtaining a Pass. Students who are able to use the given information to best effect, and who avoid inaccuracies, will achieve the higher grades of Credit and Distinction. A significant proportion of First Level candidates achieve a Credit or Distinction.

1.2 Extended Syllabus

1.2.1 Aims and objectives

The aim of this qualification is to examine the candidate's ability to understand and write basic English and use it in simple, brief business communications.

A successful candidate will demonstrate an ability to read simple business-related English texts and write clear simple English which completes a basic business task in a suitable style and layout for its intended purpose.

Objectives

A successful candidate will be able to:

- Demonstrate understanding of simple business-related communications
- Read, interpret and respond to simple business texts and data
- Adapt simple forms of office correspondence and other data to produce completed formats such as charts, tables, booking forms and report forms
- Write in continuous English simple business-style letters and memos based on given information.

Target audience

The qualification is intended for candidates who have achieved a sound basic understanding of English in a business context and an ability to use the language at a basic functional level. Candidates would be expected to be at the Council of Europe's Waystage Level or the UK National Standards (NVQ) Level 1.

Candidate progression

This qualification is intended for those who have progressed beyond the standard of English for Business Preliminary Level. It can serve as a 'bridging' course for those who wish to progress to LCCIEB Second Level in English for Business and further progress can be made up to the Third Level of this qualification.

1.2.2 Guide to assessment

Syllabus topics

The topics in the syllabus deal with the following business skills:

- Composing a simple business letter or memo
- Basic business reading comprehension
- Business information processing
- Business text and data reformulation.

In addition candidates will be expected to demonstrate a level of linguistic competence as outlined in syllabus topics 5 to 8.

Further details about the topics are given below.

Coverage of syllabus topics in the examination

There will be 4 compulsory questions corresponding to the 4 syllabus topics listed above. Questions 1 and 2 carry 30 marks each. Questions 3 and 4 carry 20 marks each.

1.3 Examination format

Candidates will be assessed via a 2-hour examination consisting of 4 questions as follows:

- Question 1 involves the composition of a letter or memo, based on given information. The content should be between 150 and 200 words. The stimulus will be rubric information giving data on which to base a reply. The content of the letter or memo will be simple business-style communication dealing with:
  - retail orders
  - customer enquiries
  - requests for information
  - replies to complaints
  - reminders about tasks in hand
  - communications between work colleagues.

- Question 2 involves understanding and responding to short passages of business-related prose of about 300 words. The stimulus for the exercise will be:
  - a passage on a business-related topic in language appropriate to the level
  - a series of statements about the content and information in the passage.

- Question 3 involves a 'read and think' comprehension test, based on some graphic or numerical display, requiring single word or single figure answers. The stimulus to the question will be data in the form of a chart or a table relating to, for example:
  - company car fleet hire charges
  - office accommodation agencies
  - conference facilities at an hotel
  - company branches and staffing details.

- Question 4 involves a 'read and write' reformulation task using data to complete forms or diagrams. The stimulus for the question will be selected from:
  - data or information in written notes
  - a conversation about a business-related situation
  - a record of a telephone, fax, or e-mail message.

1.4 Answer guidance

Each question requires an answer that is:
- correct in formal terms regarding:
  - grammar, punctuation, spelling and layout
  - good non-literary business communication at a basic level.
- appropriate in terms of:
  - adopting a simple low grade business role if required
  - fitness for the occasion and any social role required
  - displaying simple politeness in giving straightforward information or a simple opinion.
- adequate in practical business terms in the sense that:
  - the purpose of the communication is achieved
  - the task is successfully completed
  - the correct format is chosen
  - essential matters are included and dealt with

- irrelevant matter is excluded
- order, clarity, balance, and relevance are evident.

While candidates will receive credit for good grammar, accuracy, style, layout, and maturity of expression, the scope of these criteria will be limited, since comparatively little continuous prose will be demanded. Candidates will be able to display good comprehension without risking a loss of marks through poor production.

Candidates are allowed to take one dictionary into this examination which may be either English or foreign language/English; the LCCIEB cannot undertake to advise on which dictionaries to choose, and candidates make the choice entirely at their own risk. Poor quality dictionaries may be misleading, and candidates will lose time looking up words if they frequently have recourse to them.

Candidates are also recommended to refer to the Examiners' Reports and Model Answers and past question papers for English for Business First Level, which are available from the LCCIEB and which give advice on layout and presentation.

NB This guide makes use of 2 recent past papers and provides model answers and Examiner comments relevant to these 2 papers.

Varieties of English

The Board will accept any of the main varieties of English (British, North American, Australasian) in candidates' answers as long as candidates are consistent in the variety that they use.

1.5 Marking schedule

Pass mark information

Pass	50%
Credit	60%
Distinction	75%

Mark allocation

Marks are awarded for accuracy of spelling, punctuation, grammar, appropriate content, style, tone, length, format, clarity and suitability of communication.

A typical weighting of marks for a complete written paper would be:

- clarity and appropriateness of layout   20%
- style, tone, suitability to the task   30%
- content and communication of message   20%
- accuracy of grammar, spelling etc   30%

Total 100%

1.6 Useful publications

This book refers to the following LCCIEB publications, and you may find it useful to have a copy of each of these for additional guidance and information.

Note: If you are following the course at a college or university, these should be available for reference through your college tutor. Alternatively your tutor will ensure that all relevant information is given to you as part of the course. If you are using this book independently or with a friend, you will find that all the relevant information is contained in the book.

1 English for Business First Level, Extended Syllabus (January 1999). This book contains complete information about the course.

2 Examiners' Reports and Model Answers. These are available for many past papers and provide useful information about candidate performance, examination expectations, model answers for each question on the paper, and detailed information on common errors and pitfalls to avoid. You should always remember, however, that a 'model' answer represents only **one** way of answering a question, particularly in regard to continuous written English. There are an infinite number of acceptable alternatives. You should **never try** to adapt a model answer from a past paper to write an answer for the paper you are sitting.

2

How to use the Candidate's Book

2.1 Overview

The following chapters cover the Examination Question topics:

3   Business letters (Examination Question 1)

4   Memos (Examination Question 1)

5   Basic reading comprehension (Examination Question 2)

6   Information processing (Examination Question 3)

7   Text and data reformulation (Examination Question 4).

Chapter 8, Language competence, does not have a specific examination question. However, the topics covered in the chapter will help you to become more proficient in written English. To make the most of the information:

- plan your term timetable so that you cover every item in the chapter

- review chapter items to check your rough work.

2.2 Planning your time

The time you take is up to you. It depends on how fast you learn. There is no set time for the work, so do not worry if a particular chapter takes you a long time. Just make sure that you do the work carefully, and that you understand everything that you have done. However, always try to complete the exercise you are doing before you take a break.

Which chapters have the most work?

- Chapter 3 (Business letters)

- Chapter 4 (Memos)

- Chapter 5 (Basic reading comprehension)

It is in these chapters that you have the most to learn.

Letter-writing calls for many skills, so this is the longest chapter.

There are 10 sections in Chapter 3. Memos has fewer pages, but there is still a lot of work to cover. Chapter 5 also calls for careful preparation.

Chapters 6 and 7 are easier and you will not need to spend as much time on these.

Why is Chapter 3 (Business letters) so much longer than the other chapters?

- Letter-writing is the first exercise in continuous writing in the English for Business examination, and it is needed at all levels of the examination.

- There are many parts to a letter and many skills to learn.
- Because letter-writing is so important, you need to spend a lot of time building your skills and practising them with the checklists and build-up sheets.
- Much of what you learn in Business letters applies to Memos. The build-up exercises in Chapter 3 will help you complete Chapter 4.

2.3 Checklists and build-up sheets

These are used in Business letters and Memos. You will find examples of them in Chapter 9. The situations/tasks provided in Chapter 9 are similar to those on actual examination question papers and provide the basic information and material for your work. You can use the checklists and build-up sheets to prepare your letters and memos. You can compare your own with the completed letters and memos.

All the information for writing letters and memos is assembled in the checklists. As you work through the chapter, you fill in the sections of the checklists (names and addresses, opening sentences, etc). The blank checklists and letter build-up sheets that you fill in yourself are used to write the final letters and memos.

The completed checklists, build-up sheets, letters and memos are to help you to check your own work, and to make sure that you are on-track.

Each assignment in Business letters and in Memos includes a:

- situation/task
- checklist
- build-up sheet.

The checklists and build-up sheets include:

- Letter-writing checklists 1–10 (completed)
- Letter-writing checklist (blank) for you to complete
- Sample letter-writing build-up sheets for situations/tasks 1–2
- Letter-writing build-up sheets (blank) for you to complete
- Memo-writing checklists 1–10 (completed)
- Memo-writing checklist (blank) for you to complete.

When you check your work against each completed checklist, look at only those parts of the checklists that are relevant for the exercise. Cover the rest of the checklist with a sheet of paper. It is important that you produce your own answers to the exercises before reading the answers in the completed checklists.

2.4 Organising your work

Make 10 copies of each of the following:

- blank letter-writing checklist (page 119)
- blank letter-writing build-up sheet (page 122)
- blank memo-writing checklist (page 146).

You will also need a rough workbook, or single sheets of paper, for some of the exercises in the chapters. A loose-leaf binder or file will help you to keep all your work together. At the end of the course, you will then have a copy of all the work you have done. This can be used for further practice or revision before the examination.

Part 2
Extended Syllabus topics

3

Business letters

After studying this chapter and completing the exercises, you should be able to:

1 *compose a business letter using the information given in a situation/task;*

2 *adopt an appropriate style or tone;*

3 *use the conventions for layout, language and paragraphing;*

4 *display coherence and cohesion to ensure fluent reading;*

5 *avoid over-use and unnecessary copying from the situation/task;*

6 *ensure the length of the letter is adequate;*

7 *ensure that the finished letter is mailable.*

Extended Syllabus references

1.1 Compose a letter on the basis of given data with a particular aim or instruction

1.2 Adopt an appropriate style or tone for the particular purpose

1.3 Employ consistent business letter conventions regarding

    1.3.1 layout, addresses, salutation, complimentary close, and signature

    1.3.2 conventions of simple business letter language

    1.3.3 paragraphing

1.4 Display coherence and cohesion to ensure fluent reading of the letter

1.5 Avoid over-use and unnecessary copying from the rubric

1.6 Ensure that the length of the letter is adequate for the stated purpose

1.7 Ensure that the finished letter is mailable/sendable

Definition

A business letter is a formal written communication between the representatives of two organisations about a specific business matter.

Main features of a business letter:

- layout is conventional
- topic is specific
- content relates only to that topic
- style is simple and straightforward.

Some of the reasons for writing a business letter:

- respond to an inquiry
- make a complaint
- confirm attendance at a meeting
- order goods or materials.

KEYNOTES

- A business letter is a formal written communication between the representatives of two organisations about a specific business matter.
- A business letter adopts a formal approach to layout and communication.
- A business letter keeps to the purpose.
- A business letter contains no irrelevant information.

3.1 Layout

After completing this section you should know:

- names of the parts of a business letter
- standard layout.

Every business letter has the following parts:

1 Writer's address
2 Date
3 Inside address
4 Salutation
5 Body of the letter
6 Complimentary close
7 Writer's signature
8 Writer's name (printed)
9 Job title or position

See Figure 3.1, Standard business letter layout, p. 15

Figure 3.2, Sample business letter, p. 16

Writer's address

Date

Inside address

Address of the
person to whom
the letter is written.

Salutation

Body of the letter

This is the 'content' of the letter.

Complimentary close

Writer's signature

Writer's name (printed)

Job title or position

Figure 3.1   Standard business-letter layout

Acme Vacuum Cleaner Company
Fall Birch Road
Henbury
Gloucester
GL2 5ER
England

9 November 1999

Ms Janet Duxbury
District Education Officer
Atlas House
The Wellsprings
Henbury
Gloucester
GL1 3LD

Dear Ms Duxbury

I am writing to ask permission for our company to use the car park at the James North High School for a 2-week period starting on 22 December.

The reason for this request is that our own car park is due to be resurfaced and redesigned.

The work will take 2 weeks to complete, and we need a suitable car park nearby which can take a hundred cars. The school car park, which is across the road from our factory, would be perfect.

I understand that the school is on holiday during the period that we need it whilst the work is being done.

I have spoken to the Head of the school, Mrs Anne Legge, who says she is happy to help. You may know that our company employs several James North pupils every year when they leave the school. Mrs Legge did ask me to contact you, however, for official permission to use the school's car park.

I hope you will be able to give your permission, and I look forward to hearing from you.

Yours sincerely

Martha Reeve

Martha Reeve

Office Manager

Figure 3.2   Sample business letter

3.2 Addresses

Note: In modern business practice there is no punctuation (comma or full stop) in addresses.

In the examination questions UK addresses will be used.

3.2.1 Writer's address

Parts of writer's address (Figure 3.3):

1 Name of business organisation

Note: The name of the person actually writing the letter does not appear in the writer's address. This is written after the signature (Section 3.3.3).

2 Number and street OR street and number

UK	52 Railway Road
Germany	Alpenstrasse 33

3 City

4 Postcode or zipcode

This can be a combination of letters and numbers or numbers alone:

UK	N1 2LK
Canada	N2E 4M6
United States	65302-967
Germany	98617

5 Country.

Note: Organisations will usually have a printed letterhead or a computer template.

Cybergames Ltd	→	organisation
44 Regent Street	→	number and street
London	→	city
WC1 2EE	→	postcode
England	→	country

Figure 3.3   Writer's address

EXERCISE 3.1

Arrange the following writers' addresses in the correct order. It may be useful if you mark the name of the item beside each line (Figure 3.3). This will make it easier to arrange in the correct order. Answers are given in Appendix 1, page 183.

1   Bournemouth
    Peacock and Bryson
    BR1 5PW
    England
    52 Railway Road

2   2 Bank Street
    Lee's Bicycles
    BM2 3JD
    England
    Birmingham

3   London
    Eurodome Rooflights
    N15 2EL
    15 Frinton Street
    England

4   Cormack Plumbing Engineers
    London
    27 Norval Road
    N23 2LS
    England

5   London
    Martha Fashions Limited
    England
    SW14 3MT
    14 Thames Road

6   Jessica Software
    England
    35 Chestnut Avenue
    SW6 2LM
    London

3.2.2 Inside address

An exact copy of this address is written on the envelope.

Parts of inside address (Figure 3.4):

1 Name of person you are writing to (addressee)

2 Job title of person.

Note: This is the difference between the inside address and the writer's address (Section 3.2.1). Name and job title are not part of the writer's address.

3 Name of organisation

4 Number and street (see Section 3.2.1)

5 City

6 Postcode or zipcode (see Section 3.2.1)

7 Country.

Mr Roland Jenks	→	addressee
Sales Director	→	job title
Business Lines Ltd	→	organisation
2 Bridge Street	→	number and street
Oxford	→	city
OX2 4JF	→	postcode
England	→	country
Dear Mr Jenks	→	salutation

Figure 3.4   Inside address and salutation

EXERCISE 3.2

Arrange the following inside addresses in the correct order. You may find it useful if you mark the name of the item beside each line. This will make it easier to arrange in the correct order (Figure 3.4). Answers are given in Appendix 1, pages 183–4.

1 Managing Director
   Ms Ruth Bailey
   47 Franklin Avenue
   London
   Stratton Cycles
   England
   SE22 5US

2 19 Woburn Terrace
   Chief Accountant
   London
   James Elliot
   E8 2ML
   Thompson Electrical Goods
   England

3 England
   Andrew Forsythe
   Bristol
   Victoria Yachts
   Design Department
   17 Golders Quay
   B43 4NW

4 Carol Browne
   537 Girton Road
   Managing Director
   London
   Harvester Enterprises
   England
   N23 45US

5 Morden Publishers
   Mrs Nancy Lorimer
   72 Finchley Gardens
   London
   Editorial Department
   SW11 2RL
   England

6 John Burns
   89 Surrey Way
   Cambridge
   Alpha Security
   Managing Director
   CB45 8LK
   England

7 Chief Buyer Link Fashion House Miss Florence Lees OX56 7PM 92 Semple Way Oxford England	8 Saunders Toys Desmond Fitzgerald 17 Nicholson Road Chief Designer Leeds L54 9TR England

Before you attempt the following exercises, make sure you have made 10 copies of the blank checklist on page 119 in the Resources section.

When you check your work against each completed checklist, look at only those parts of the checklists that are relevant for the exercise. Cover the rest of the checklist with a sheet of paper. It is important that you produce your own answers to the exercises before reading the answers in the completed checklist.

EXERCISE 3.3

1   Look at letter-writing situation/task 1 on page 105 of the Resources section. You will find examples similar to this on the First Level English for Business examination paper. They contain the situations that you are asked to write a letter about.

2   Read situation/task 1 carefully, then in your workbook write out in full:

- the writer's address for the question
- the inside address for the question.

3   Check your work carefully to make sure it is correct. If you need to, remind yourself about the address rules on pages 17–18.

4   Turn to the letter-writing situation checklist on page 109 in the Resources section. Use your blank piece of card or paper to cover the rest of the checklist. At the top of the checklist you will find the correct versions for the two addresses you have just written in your workbook. Are they the same as yours? If they are, very well done. If they are not, why is this? For example:

- did you forget to include Mr Roland Jenks and start the inside address with 'Sales Director'?
- did you include the position of Assistant Sales Manager in the writer's address?
- did you read without proper care and put Ms Pauline Davi in one of the two addresses?

If you did make any mistakes in Exercise 3.3, look again at the rules on pages 17–18, and make sure you know what you did wrong.

EXERCISE 3.4

1   Look at letter-writing situations/tasks 2 to 5 on pages 105–6.

2   In your workbook write the correct writers' and inside addresses for each of these.

3   Check them carefully.

4   Now check them all against the correct versions which appear on the completed checklists on pages 110–13 of the Resources section.

5   Did you get them all right? If you did, well done! If not, look carefully to find out what mistakes you made. Make sure you understand your mistakes before you carry on.

6   When you are happy that they are all correct, and you understand why, copy each of the addresses for letter-writing situations/tasks 1 to 5 onto your blank checklists.

Note: The blank checklists for letters and memos will form your own record of work done in these sections. They will finally be used to write letters and memos which satisfy the examination criteria. Always remember to work in your workbook and get things all correct before you fill in a section of your checklist.

EXERCISE 3.5

This exercise completes this section.

1 Look at letter-writing situations/tasks 6 to 10 on pages 107–8 of the Resources section.

2 In your workbook write for each situation/task:
  - the writer's address
  - the inside address.

3 Check your work using the completed checklists on pages 114–18 as before. If everything is correct, enter all the addresses onto your own blank checklists for each situation. Well done!

KEYNOTES

- The correct order for an address is: name of person, number and street, town or city, postcode (zipcode), country.
- The writer's address is the address of the person writing the letter.
- The inside address is the address of the person receiving the letter.
- The writer's address is placed above the date.
- The writer's address never starts with a person's name.
- The writer's address always starts with the name of a company or a department.
- The inside address is placed below the date.
- The inside address always starts with the name or position of the person receiving the letter.
- It is now accepted practice NOT to use punctuation throughout the layout of a business letter. This practice is recommended by LCCIEB.

3.3 Salutation, complimentary close and signature

After carefully studying this section you should be able to:

- Choose the appropriate salutation
- Add a complimentary close
- End with the correct signature.

3.3.1 Salutation

The form used as the opening in a business letter. The first word is always 'Dear', followed by the name of the person to whom you are writing (see Figure 3.4, p. 18).

3.3.1.1 Addressee is a man

- Name: John Reynolds

  Salutation: Dear Mr Reynolds

- Job title (for example, Branch Manager) known but not person's name. You do know that the Branch Manager is a man.

  Salutation: Dear Sir

3.3.1.2 Addressee is a woman

- Name: Mrs Janet Jones

  Salutation: Dear Mrs Jones

- Name: Miss Mary Robinson

  Salutation: Dear Miss Robinson

- Name: Ms Celia Strong

  Salutation: Dear Ms Strong

- Name: Joan Keane

  Salutation: Dear Ms Keane

- Job title (for example, Managing Director) known but not name. You do know that the Managing Director is a woman.

  Salutation: Dear Madam

3.3.2 Complimentary close (Figure 3.5)

This serves the same purpose as 'Goodbye'. Use:

- 'Yours sincerely' when you address the person by name

- 'Yours faithfully' when you address the person as 'Dear Madam' or 'Dear Sir'.

3.3.3 Signature (Figure 3.5)

This should consist of:

- Written signature of person writing letter
- Name
- Job title.

Yours sincerely	→	complimentary close
Janet Burns	→	writer's signature
Janet Burns	→	writer's name
Assistant Manager	→	job title

Figure 3.5   Complimentary close and signature

EXERCISE 3.6

1 Read the 10 letter-writing situations/tasks on pages 105–8.
2 Choose the appropriate salutation and complimentary close for each one.
3 Write your answers in the table overleaf.

Situation no	Correct salutation	Correct complimentary close
1		
2		
3		
4		
5		
6		
7		
8		
9		
10		

4   Now compare your answers with the table in Appendix 1, page 184. Are they all correct?

5   Enter the correct salutations and complimentary closes on your own letter-writing situation/task checklists.

KEYNOTES

- The salutation is the correct term for saying 'hello' in a business letter.
- The complimentary close is the correct term for saying 'goodbye' in a business letter.
- If you know the name of the person, you write 'Dear Mr Smith . . . Yours sincerely'.
- If you do not know the name, you write 'Dear Sir (or Dear Madam) . . . Yours faithfully'.
- If you do not know if a female is married or not, you write 'Dear Ms Smith . . . Yours sincerely'.
- You must never write the full name of the person (e.g. Dear John Smith).

3.4 Revision test

You have now learned about the layout of a business letter:

- addresses (Section 3.2)
- salutation (Section 3.3.1)
- complimentary close (Section 3.3.2)
- signature (Section 3.3.3).

The revision test gives you an opportunity to check your knowledge of these parts of a business letter.

You should:

- aim to complete the test in 30 minutes;
- write your answers in your workbook;
- check your answers against the answers given in Appendix 1, pages 184–5;
- if you have made a mistake, review the section and do that part of the test again.

QUESTION 1

Write the following mixed-up addresses in the correct order.

Mixed-up address	Correct address
Blackburn 654 Somerset Road England Mrs P Horrocks BB4 7PD	
Novi Sad 4000 Ms Jelena Pavlovic Franca Rosamana 16 Jugoslavia	
France 16 Avenue des Abeilles Belleville Henri Charot Wines Ltd Mr Jean Aruvée	

QUESTION 2

Write the correct salutation and complimentary close for the following situations:

Situation	Salutation	Complimentary close
A letter to the Senior Accountant at Brands Ltd		
A reply to a letter from Helena Moore at A1 Films		
A request from the Chief Buyer (a man) at Alamo Sports		
A letter of thanks to Mr Rex Lee at United Biscuits		
A letter to Anisha Sidat, the MD of Suncare Ltd		

QUESTION 3

Add the 5 missing items to the following letter:

The Hong Kong Packing Co

1 _____

2 _____

TB1 4ED
England

30 April 2000

The Marketing Director
TDD Engineering Ltd

3 _____

London
SE4 4EB

4 _____

We received your quotation for a contract to service all our vehicles. This is now being considered with other quotations. We shall contact you in due course.

Thank you for being so prompt in sending the information.

5 _____

Wang Rongshun

Wang Rongshun
(Assistant Manager)

QUESTION 4

Identify and write down the 5 mistakes in the following letter:

The Pet Shop
Swindon
SD1 4JB
6 Brandon Street

2001 January 6

Ms Andrea kostellanos
64 Buckfield Lane
Swindon
SD3 6PJ

Dear Madam

We are still waiting for payment for the three kittens you ordered from us. Please send this as soon as possible. Our terms are cash in advance for all animal orders.

Yours truthfully

J Treherne

J Treherne
Proprietor

Mistakes

1 _____

2 _____

3 _____

4 _____

5 _____

QUESTION 5

You work as Assistant Manager for Top Class Papers Ltd and your head office is at:

82 Plaza Gardens, Ho Chi Minh City, Vietnam.

You have received a letter from the Stock Controller of Foursquare Books Ltd. His address is:

67 East 55th Street, New York 65307, USA.

The letter asks for a price list of your available papers.

Lay out the writer's and inside addresses, date, salutation, complimentary close, signature and job title for a letter of reply. Do not write the body of the letter.

Answers are given in Appendix 1, pages 184–5.

Remember: The purpose of this test is to identify the items in Sections 3.2 and 3.3 which you understand and those which require further study. Complete the test before you look at the answers.

You have now completed the first part of letter-writing.

There are 30 marks in total for the letter/memo question.

Layout   5 marks

Content   15 marks

Style/Tone 4 marks

Accuracy   6 marks (a half mark deducted for each error of spelling, grammar, and punctuation)

If you write a letter of the required length (150–200 words) and you make no errors in spelling, grammar and punctuation, you can expect 6 more marks. The mark for style and tone depends on how well you match the wording of your letter to the task. For example, is it business-like and informative, with short, clear sentences? There are 4 more marks to be picked up here. With care and attention to these areas, you can gain half of the 30 marks before the content of your letter is taken into account. Even with a few errors, you need only 4 or 5 points to bring your mark up to the pass standard. If your letter is short, this will affect the marks you are awarded in each area. But, if the length is right, you are halfway to a pass if the areas mentioned are properly dealt with.

If you remember that all the information you need for a pass is in the situation at the start of the question, you have only to put that information in a sensible order and make no errors, and you are at the pass mark. For a mark in the Credit and Distinction ranges you will need to fulfil the length requirement completely (150–200 words) and show some flair and imagination to 'lift' your letter above the ordinary pass standard.

It is most important to achieve a correct layout in your letters. A good start with the layout gives you some easy marks in Examination Question 1. The letter or memo is worth 30 marks in the examination. Marks are given for:

- layout
- content
- style and tone
- accuracy.

Up to 5 marks are given for correct layout of the letter or memo.

If you:

- write a letter of the required length (150-200 words)
- and make no errors in spelling, grammar and punctuation

you can expect up to 5 or 6 more marks for **accuracy**.

You gain more marks for **style and tone**. If you match the wording of your letter to the task (is it, for example, business-like and informative, with short clear sentences?), you will gain 3 or 4 marks. The point is that if you take care in these parts of your letter (or memo) writing, you can gain up 9 or 12 marks, *before* the content of your letter is assessed. You therefore need only 4 or 5 points to bring you up to the pass standard. A short letter will, of course, reduce the marks you are awarded in each area. You must write between 150 and 200 words.

Remember that all the information you need is given in the situation/task. If you put that information in a logical order, and make no errors, you are at the pass mark. For a Credit or Distinction, you will need a letter of 150–200 words, standard layout, well written and appropriate to the task.

Sections 3.5 to 3.10 will teach you how to break down the content element of the letter and provide an easy system for success. Remember that what you write must always depend on the information in the situation/task for the question. If you read and interpret the situation/task carefully and correctly, you will be able to decide on the content.

3.5 Main subject matter

The main body of a business letter has three parts:

1 Introductory paragraph
2 Central core: what the letter must do (usually 2 to 4 paragraphs)
3 Concluding paragraph.

After carefully studying this section you should be able to:

* analyse the information given in letter-writing situations/tasks
* decide on the main subject
* arrange details in logical order
* write a complete letter.

3.5.1 Sample letter-writing situation/task: how to assign details to correct part of letter

In the exercises and examination questions, the situation and the task appear as separate paragraphs. We suggest that you write the essential information in each sentence on a separate line. This will make it easier for you to decide how to order the information.

Situation: You are the Assistant Maintenance Manager for Benwell's Garden Supplies, 402 Market Place, Leeds L24 SW5. You have received a letter from Powertools Ltd which manufactures industrial lawn mowers. They supply you with their petrol-driven model, the Marathon M162P. The letter informs you about a possible fault in the fuel system of the M162P. They recommend that you recall all of the Marathons you have sold in order to carry out a safety check in Benwell's workshop. You have sold two M162P Marathons to the Leeds Department of Parks and Gardens.

Situation: essential information

Assistant Maintenance Manager, Benwell's Garden Supplies, Leeds

Powertools Ltd manufacturers of industrial lawn mowers

Suppliers of petrol-driven lawn mowers, Marathon M162P

Possible fault in the fuel system of the M162P

Recommend you recall in order to carry out a safety check in your workshop

Benwell's has sold two Marathons to Leeds Parks and Gardens Department

Additional information

Benwell's address is 402 Market Place, Leeds L24 SW5

Assume that you are Benwell's Assistant Maintenance Manager

Use today's date

Task: Write a letter to the Director of Parks and Gardens, Town Hall, Civic Centre, Leeds L15 2W. Explain the problem and ask him to make an appointment by telephone to arrange a safety check for the mowers.

Task: essential information

Letter to Director of Parks and Gardens, Town Hall, Civic Centre, Leeds L15 2W

Explain the problem with the Marathon mowers

Ask him to make an appointment by telephone to arrange a safety check

Essential information: combined list

- Copy the essential information from the situation and task
- Underline the important points
- Make a list of the points.

Example of a combined list of essential information

Assistant Maintenance Manager, Benwell's Garden Supplies, Leeds

<u>Letter from Powertools Ltd</u> manufacturers of <u>industrial lawn mower, model Marathon M162P</u>

<u>Possible fault in the fuel system</u> of the M162P

<u>Recommend you recall</u> in order to carry out a <u>safety check in your workshop</u>

Benwell's has sold two Marathons to Leeds Parks and Gardens Department

Additional information

Benwell's address is 402 Market Place, Leeds L24 SW5

Letter to Director of Parks and Gardens, Town Hall, Civic Centre, Leeds L15 2W

<u>Explain the problem</u> with the Marathon mowers

Ask him to <u>make an appointment by telephone</u> to <u>arrange a safety check</u>

List the underlined points:

1 Letter from Powertools Ltd
2 Industrial lawn mowers
3 Possible fault in fuel system, model Marathon M162P
4 Recommend recall
5 Safety check in workshop
6 Explain the problem
7 Make an appointment by telephone.

Write down in your workbook:

1 Writer's address
2 Inside address
3 Salutation
4 Complimentary close
5 Signature.

Read carefully and decide precisely what the main subject matter should be.

We need to identify the subject matter correctly and precisely because:

- the main subject matter will form the core of the letter
- it will help us to plan the writing of the letter

- it will help us to put the details in a logical order
- it will be a guide if we add other details that are not in the situation.

Now read the following short letter text.

> Thank you for your order. At the moment we have none of the items you want in stock. We expect a delivery some time next week. I suggest you telephone next week to check the situation. Please do not telephone before 3.00 pm, as we are very busy.

What is the main subject matter here? Is it:

- items of stock not available?
- a request for an afternoon phone call?
- pointing out that the firm is a busy one?

Use the same process of underlining the important points to help you to decide.

The simple answer is: the first option. You are writing to say there are no items in stock; all the other points depend on this fact to make sense. If the stock was available:

- you would not be saying a delivery was expected
- you would not be asking the customer to telephone next week.

3.5.2 Exercises

EXERCISE 3.7

Look at letter-writing situations/tasks 1 to 4 on pages 105–6.

Read each situation and task carefully.

In your workbook write down what you think is the main subject matter of each letter. **Use the underlining and listing technique to help you.** Write each one down as a sentence beginning:

The main subject matter for situation 1

is _____

Remember that you can test your decision by asking yourself the following.

- Will this form the core of the letter?
- Is it really the main reason for the letter being sent?
- Does this help me to put the letter in order?
- Does this help me to place the details?
- Will added detail about this subject improve the letter?

When you have written your answers, compare them with the model answers on the completed letter-writing situations/task checklists on pages 109–12.

How successful were you? The words you have used will be different, but have you chosen the *correct topic* for each situation?

If your answer is similar in content to the model answer, enter **your answers** on your blank checklists for each of situations/tasks 1 to 4.

EXERCISE 3.8

Follow the same procedure for situations 5 to 10.

Write your answers first in your workbook.

Compare your answers with the model answers on the completed checklists on pages 113–18.

If they are similar, enter **your answers** onto your blank checklists.

KEYNOTES

- Read the situation/task very carefully.
- Decide what the letter is really about.
- Use coloured pens to underline the important points and make a list of these.
- Decide which point is the most important; all other points depend on this one.
- The main subject matter is the *core* of the letter.
- The main subject matter helps you to plan and put the letter in logical order.
- The main subject matter helps you to invent appropriate and relevant details of your own.

3.6 Key points, additional details and additional invented details

After carefully studying this section, you should be able to:

- Identify the key points in a situation/task
- Use the main subject and key points to make a framework for the letter
- Identify the additional details and add to the framework
- Create additional invented details and add to the framework
- Use a letter-writing build-up sheet to write 3 basic letters:
  1 Using the main subject and key points
  2 Using the main subject, key points and additional details
  3 Using the main subject, key points, additional details and additional invented details.

3.6.1 Review of Benwell's Garden Supplies situation/task (Section 3.5)

Re-read Section 3.5 and review that section in your workbook.

The main subject matter is 'possible fault in fuel system'.

3.6.2 Identify key points and list in logical order

EXERCISE 3.9

Underline the key points in the Benwell's situation/task.

Make a list in your workbook.

Check your list against this model answer.

> - Letter from Powertools Ltd
> - Marathon lawn mower (model M162P)
> - Possible fault in the fuel system
> - All models M162P are being recalled
> - Safety check in workshop
> - Make an appointment

Note: You may have used different words. That doesn't matter as long as your list contains the same key points.

EXERCISE 3.10

Arrange the key points in the most logical order. Remember to include the main subject 'possible fault in fuel system'. Number each item.

Check your list against this model answer.

> 1 Letter from Powertools Ltd
> 2 Lawn mower Marathon (model M162P)
> 3 Possible fault in fuel system
> 4 All models recalled
> 5 For safety check in workshop
> 6 Make an appointment

3.6.3 Write a basic letter

Link the key points together in a few short sentences.

Remember that this is only your first draft.

> Model basic letter
>
> **1** We have received a letter from Powertools Ltd **2** about the Marathon lawn mower (model M162P). **3** There is a possible fault in the fuel system. **4** All models are recalled for a safety check. **5** This will take place in our workshop. **6** Please make an appointment.

- this is a simple basic letter
- it includes the key points from the situation
- it is to the point and business-like.

This letter contains approximately 50 words. To obtain maximum marks on Examination Question 1 your letter must contain between 150 and 200 words. When you include additional details and additional invented details, your letter will approach the right length.

3.6.4 List additional details and rewrite basic letter

EXERCISE 3.11

Make a list in your workbook of possible additional details and compare it with following list.

1 Just received

2 Make industrial lawn mowers

3 Petrol-driven lawn mower

4 Recommend recall

5 Two sold to Leeds Parks and Gardens Department

6 Telephone

EXERCISE 3.12

Rewrite the basic letter (Section 3.6.3) using the additional details. Compare it with the model letter below. Additional details are printed in **bold**.

We have **just received** a letter from Powertools Ltd who **make industrial lawn mowers** and supply us with the **petrol-driven** Marathon **lawn mower** (model M162P). Powertools say there is a possible fault in the fuel system. They **recommend** that all models are **recalled** for a safety check. This will take place in our workshop. **We have sold you 2 of these lawn mowers**. Please **telephone** to make an appointment with us.

In this version we have used 73 words. This is half-way to the 150–200 asked for in the examination. We have used the information in the situation/task to reach this point. If you read carefully, and use the information in correct order, you can do this with every letter-writing situation/task.

3.6.5 List additional invented details and rewrite letter

EXERCISE 3.13

Look again at the Benwell's Garden Supplies situation/task.

Below the task is the following statement:

'You may invent any details that you think are necessary.'

Write down a list of 4 or 5 details that you think will fit the situation. Compare your list with the one supplied below.

What details did you invent? Did you include something about:

• your firm, Benwell's?

• Powertools Ltd?

• the Marathon?

- the problem?
- the recall?
- the safety check?
- your workshop?
- the appointment?

Details about any of these would be acceptable.

Think about these examples:

- Benwell's   'we take pride in our after-sales service'
- Powertools Ltd   'the leading lawn mower manufacturers'
- The Marathon   'best selling, reliable industrial mower'
- The problem   'involves the feed pipe in the engine'
- The recall   'within the next two weeks'
- The safety check   'at no cost to yourselves'
- Your workshop   'fully equipped for maintenance'
- The appointment   'priority for valuable customers'.

EXERCISE 3.14

Now let us add 4 or 5 of these 'additional invented details' to the letter.

Do it yourself first with the details you thought of.

When you have finished, compare your letter with the one below.

We have just received a letter from Powertools Ltd, the **leading lawn mower manufacturers**. They supply us with the **best selling, reliable** petrol-driven Marathon **industrial mower** (model M162P). Powertools say that there is a possible fault in the fuel system, which **involves the feed pipe in the engine**. They recommend that all models are recalled for a safety check. This will take place in our fully equipped workshop **at no cost to yourselves**. We have sold you 2 of these mowers. You know we **take pride in our after-sales service**. Please telephone to make a **priority** appointment with us for the check.

(102 words)

We have increased the letter to just over 100 words. It was not a difficult task. The letter is still short of the required 150 to 200 words, but if the layout and accuracy were good, the letter would gain enough marks to be close to a pass in an examination.

In this section we have:

- composed a basic letter using **key points**
- included **additional details** from the situation/task and rewritten the letter
- included **additional invented details** and rewritten the letter.

In the next section we will use this method with letter-writing situations 1 to 3 in the same way.

KEYNOTES

- The key points are the most important points in the letter.
- Underline the key points in the situation/task.
- Write the key points as a list.
- Key points do not include the writer's or the inside names or addresses.
- Write out the key points in 2 or 3 short sentences; this gives you the basic letter.

3.7 Exercises

In this section you will prepare a letter for letter-writing situations/tasks 3 to 10 using:

- main subject and key points
- additional details
- additional invented details.

This section continues the process of writing business letters as outlined in the Extended Syllabus topics 1.3.1 and 1.3.2.

Follow the steps you used in Section 3.6 for letter-writing situations/tasks 1 and 2. The only difference is that no completed build-up sheets are given. Create your own on the photocopies you have made of the blank build-up sheet.

EXERCISE 3.15

Using main subject and key points

Remember that you have already decided on the main subject for each situation/task and copied it onto the checklist in the box 'main subject'.

1 Underline the key points in the situation/task text.

2 List the key points in your workbook.

3 Arrange the key points in logical order. Remember to include the main subject in the list.

4 Compare your list with the completed checklist.

5 Add any essential points from the checklist that you have missed.

6 Copy your list onto your own checklist.

7 Write a basic letter in your workbook using the key points.

8 Make any changes that you think will improve your letter.

9 Copy your basic letter onto your build-up sheet.

EXERCISE 3.16

Using main subject, key points, additional details

Follow steps 1 to 10 for Basic letter 1 using main subject, key points and additional details in your letter

Using main subject, key points, additional details and additional invented details

EXERCISE 3.17

1 Create a list in your workbook of invented details that you think will fit the situation and make the letter more interesting.

2 Compare your list with the one on the checklist.

3 Make any changes to your list that you think will improve your letter.

4 Copy the list onto your checklist.

5 Write a basic letter in your workbook using main subject, key points, additional points and additional invented points.

6 Make any changes that you think will improve your letter.

7 Copy your letter onto your build-up sheet.

Follow the same procedure for the 10 letter-writing situations/tasks.

When you have done the work above you will have completed:

- the sections for **key points, additional details and the additional invented details** on all 10 of your blank situation/task checklists
- all 3 sections of each of your 10 build-up sheets (the **key points** letter, the **additional details** letter, and the **additional invented details** letter).

EXERCISE 3.18

If you look at your own letter-writing checklists you will see that the Layout sections at the top are all completed. This was work that you did in the earlier chapters. Now it is time to use it again.

In the middle of a clean page in your workbook write out the **additional invented details letter** for letter-writing situation/task 1. You will find this in the bottom section of your letter-writing build-up sheet for situation/task 1.

From your letter-writing checklists for situation/task 1 add the following parts of the letter layout:

- the writer's address
- the date
- the inside address
- the salutation
- the complimentary close
- your signature.

If you are not sure where to put these on the page, use the letter layout diagram in Section 3. (Figure 3.1) on page 15.

What you should see in front of you is a **complete basic letter** for situation/task 1.

Your letter should look like Figure 3.6. This letter makes use of the completed build-up sheet and the completed checklist for situation/task 1.

Note: You could do this for all 10 letter-writing situations if you wish. It shows you how all the work you have done on writing business letters is starting to come together. The next 3 sections will show you how to make your letters even better.

Cybergames Ltd
44 Regent Street
London
WC1 2EE

1 March 2000

Mr Roland Jenks
Sales Director
Business Lines Ltd
2 Bridge Street
Oxford
OX2 4JF

Dear Mr Jenks

We are holding a demonstration of our new business games. The games are 'Takeover' and 'Marketing Manager'. This will take place at our head office on 26 March starting at 10.00 am. Our Chief Designer will be present. Special customers only are invited.

The timetable includes reception and coffee, introduction of games, hands-on testing, questions and lunch.

'Takeover' presents all the problems of taking over a company. 'Marketing Manager' contains the methods for success in positive team building.

We hope you can attend.

Yours sincerely

Jane Doe

Jane Doe
Assistant Manager

Figure 3.6   Complete basic letter, situation/task 1

KEYNOTES

- Additional details are the minor points in the situation/task.
- Write these down as a list.
- Add these to your basic letter.
- Additional invented details are the details that you supply.
- Additional invented details are always relevant to the situation/task.
- Additional invented details 'add' to the content of your letter.
- You can add these to the existing letter.

3.8 Opening and closing sentences

After studying this section you should be able to compose opening and closing sentences.

This section continues the process of writing business letters as outlined in the Extended Syllabus topics 1.3.1 and 1.3.2.

3.8.1 Opening sentences

An opening sentence should be based on:

- Purpose of the letter
- Relationship of the writer and addressee
- Main subject.

It should be polite and business-like.

EXERCISE 3.19

Compose an opening sentence for each of the following situations and write them in your workbook.

(a) A reply to a customer who has not received an order.

(b) A letter to a client about a special offer.

(c) A letter to your manager about a course on which you have been offered a place.

When you have written your sentences, compare them with the following list.

Here are some examples of opening sentences for the situations above. Which do you think is best for each situation?

(a) (i) We are sorry to hear about your missing order.

  (ii) We have no idea what has happened to your order.

  (iii) Why are you wasting our time about your order?

(b) (i) What do you think about this for a special offer?

  (ii) Yet another special offer is on its way to you.

  (iii) I am writing to let you know about our special offer.

(c) (i) Do you remember that course you said I could go on?

  (ii) I have got a place on that course – starts next week!

  (iii) I have been offered a place on the course I applied for.

You should have selected (a) (i), (b) (ii), (c) (iii).

Remember, a good opening sentence:

- suits the purpose
- is business-like
- is polite
- leads into the main subject matter
- is usually short.

Never put too much detail into an opening sentence.

Read this example of an opening sentence:

> We are extremely sorry and disturbed to hear that you have not renewed your order for 1,500 fluffy white rabbits, manufactured by the well-known firm of Trubshawe and Sons at their factory in Stoke.

This opening sentence is too long. Many of the details belong in the body of the letter.

A better opening sentence would be

> We are sorry that you have not renewed your order for fluffy white rabbits.

EXERCISE 3.20

Read letter-writing situation/task 1 (page 105) carefully.

Write a suitable opening sentence in your workbook.

Compare what you have written with the opening sentence on the completed letter-writing situation checklist on page 109.

Is your opening sentence similar?

Is it short, business-like, polite?

Does it lead into the main subject matter of a demonstration of new business games?

If your sentence does these 3 things, then write it on your situation/task checklist in the space for Opening Sentence.

Copy the sentence into each of the 3 boxes on your build-up sheet.

EXERCISE 3.2.I

Write opening sentences for letter-writing situations/tasks 2 to 10

Use a separate page in your workbook for each letter.

Copy the sentence into each of the 3 boxes on your build-up sheet.

Write down:

- main purpose
- your own opening sentence
- the opening sentence from the completed checklist.

Compare the two opening sentences.

Make any changes you think will improve your letter.

Write your opening sentence onto your own checklist sheet in the space marked Opening Sentence.

Write your opening sentence onto your letter-writing build-up sheet.

Write the sentence in **above the first sentence** of the **Additional Invented Details** letter. This is the bottom section of the build-up sheet.

KEY NOTES

The opening sentence should:

- Be relevant to the situation/task.
- Depend on who the letter is written to.
- Depend on the purpose of the letter.
- Introduce the main subject matter.
- Reflect the writer/addressee relationship.
- Be polite and business-like.
- Be fairly short.

3.8.2 Closing sentences

A closing sentence needs to:

- Be short
- Leave the reader feeling satisfied
- Have a purpose
  - express thanks or good wishes
  - suggest a future contact
- Refer to the main content.

Note: *Never* put important information in the closing sentence.

EXERCISE 3.22

Read letter-writing situation/task 1 on page 105. The main purpose of this letter (completed checklist, page 109) is:

> To ensure the attendance of Mr Jenks at the demonstration.

Write down in your workbook a suitable closing sentence.

Compare your sentence with the one on the completed checklist (page 109).

I look forward to the pleasure of seeing you at the demonstration.

This is a good closing sentence:

- It is short – 12 words
- It leaves the reader feeling satisfied – letter is positive
- It has a purpose – suggests a future contact
- Refers to the main content – the demonstration.

Make any changes to your sentence that you think will improve it.

Copy your sentence onto your checklist.

EXERCISE 3.23

Write closing sentences for letter-writing situations/tasks 2 to 10

Use a separate page in your workbook for each letter.

Write down:

- Main purpose
- Your own closing sentence
- Closing sentence from the completed checklist.

Compare the 2 closing sentences.

Make any changes you think will improve your sentence.

Write your closing sentence onto your own checklist.

Do this for each of the situations/tasks 2–10. Copy your closing sentences into the 3 boxes on your letter-writing build-up sheet.

KEYNOTES

The closing sentence should:

- Be quite short.
- Be polite and business-like.
- Leave the reader of the letter 'satisfied'.
- Have a purpose (saying goodbye, indicating future contact, etc).
- NOT contain important information.

3.9 Style and tone

After carefully studying this section, you should be able to improve the content of a basic letter by paying attention to its style and tone.

You will be able to complete the Style and Tone sections in the checklists for letter-writing situations/tasks 1 to 10.

This section continues the process of writing business letters as outlined in the Extended Syllabus topics 1.3.1 and 1.3.2.

> Style: the way of writing a letter as distinct from the content of the letter.

> Tone: the general quality or character of the letter which indicates the attitude of the writer and the relationship of the writer to the addressee.

3.9.1 Review and analysis of a basic letter

Read the letter of invitation (Figure 3.7 p. 42) carefully (letter-writing situation/task 1).

Length: approximately 90 words

Note that it follows the rules you have learned about:

- Layout, including opening and closing sentences.
- Grammar and spelling.
- Necessary information, in this case about:
  - the venue
  - the timetable
  - the games you are promoting.

The purpose of the letter is to make sure that Mr Jenks accepts the invitation to the games demonstration.

EXERCISE 3.24

What could you add to the letter to make it more confident and inviting?

Make a list of your ideas in your workbook.

Read the following suggestions:

1 history of Cybergames Ltd
2 previous visits
3 other people invited
4 new business games
5 last year's profits
6 how pleased you will be to see him
7 how enjoyable the demonstration will be

8   cost of demonstration

9   Cybergames staff at the demonstration

10   details of the timetable.

Cybergames Ltd
44 Regent Street
London
WC1 2EE

1 March 2000

Mr Roland Jenks
Sales Director
Business Lines Ltd
2 Bridge Street
Oxford
OX2 4JF

Dear Mr Jenks

I write to invite you to the launch of our latest business games.

We are holding a demonstration of our new business games. The games are 'Takeover'
and 'Marketing Manager'. This will take place at our head office on 26 March starting at
10.00 am. Our Chief Designer will be present. Special customers only are invited.

The timetable includes reception and coffee, introduction of games, hands-on testing,
questions and lunch.

'Takeover' presents all the problems of taking over a company.

'Marketing Manager' contains the methods for success in positive team building.

We hope you can attend.

Yours sincerely

Jane Doe

Jane Doe
Assistant Manager

Figure 3.7   Letter, situation/task 1: additional details and additional invented details

List in your workbook the items that probably would not interest Mr Jenks.

Compare with the following list:

1   history of Cybergames

2   his previous visits

5   last year's profits

8   cost of demonstration.

The remaining items can be divided into two lists:

- style
- tone.

Here are the two lists with suggested words and phrases to improve style and tone.

Style

  4   Games: learn a lot from both games
  9   Other staff attending: Chief Designer, Ms Pauline Davi
10   Timetable details: buffet lunch.

Tone

3   Other people invited: most valued customers, exclusive occasion
6   How pleased you will be to see him: look forward to the pleasure
7   How enjoyable the demonstration will be: and at the same time enjoyable

Read the basic letter on page 42 again. Now read the model letter on page 44 (new phrases are in **bold**).

This version of letter-writing situation/task 1 fulfils the requirements of Examination Question 1.

Remember that Mr Jenks is a businessman; he does not have time to waste.

For this reason points 1, 2, 5 and 8 are really of no interest to him. Do you agree?

On the other hand, points 3, 4, 6, 7, 9 and 10 may be of interest to him.

- He will be interested in the kind of people who will attend.
- He will want to know more about the 2 games.
- He will be pleased to know that you look forward to his company.
- He will be glad to know that he will enjoy the demonstration.
- He will be interested to know which staff are attending.
- He will want to know about the timetable.

These are the areas that he will respond to, if they are included in the letter.

EXERCISE 3.25

In your workbook write down suitable words or phrases to describe:

- the kind of people invited
- the 2 games
- how pleased you will be to see him
- how enjoyable the demonstration will be
- other staff attending the demonstration
- the timetable.

When you have finished, compare your words and phrases with the list below.

If your words and phrases are similar, and they fit into the letter, write them on your checklist in the space at the bottom labelled **suitable phrases.**

Dear Mr Jenks

As you are one of our **most valued customers**, I am writing to invite you to the demonstration of our latest computer business games.

For **special customers like yourself** we are holding a half-day demonstration of our new games, 'Takeover' and 'Marketing Manager'. This **important occasion** will be on the morning of 26 March, starting at 10.00 am. Our Chief Designer, **Ms Pauline Davi,** will open the demonstration.

The timetable for the morning is as follows:

10.00 am   Arrival and coffee.

10.30 am   Introduction to the new games by **Ms Davi**.

11.00 am   'Hands-on' testing session and questions.

12.00 pm   **Buffet** lunch.

'Takeover' is a game which presents the player with all the problems of taking over a company. 'Marketing Manager' involves the player in all the methods for positive team building and success in marketing. I am sure you will **learn a lot from** both games, and find them, at the same time, **very enjoyable.**

I **look forward to the pleasure** of seeing you at the demonstration.

Yours sincerely

Figure 3.8   Letter, situation/task 1: style and tone

Note: Length approximately 160 words

Here is the list of phrases from the completed checklist. If you think they are better than your phrases, write them on your own checklist.

- important occasion
- most valued customers
- sure you will enjoy
- learn a lot from both games
- and at the same time enjoyable
- look forward to the pleasure

EXERCISE 3.26

Read letter-writing situation/task 2 on page 105.

Here is Basic letter 3 from the build-up sheet.

We request space and accommodation for the Summer Furniture Exhibition. We need 5 display areas – 3 areas for living rooms and 2 areas for bedrooms – and an office area for 3 staff. We need a lighting technician. We also need accommodation for 2 nights for 2 persons.

We attended last year and several orders were taken. We are looking for more new customers.

Invoice our Accounts Department. Send early confirmation.

Figure 3.9   Basic letter, situation/task 2

This is a basic letter. You need to improve the style and tone.

Follow these steps:

- Read the situation/task again (page 105).
- Review the main subject on the checklist.
- Consider the content so far.
- Review the relationship between the writer and the person the letter is written to.
- Write down suitable words and phrases in your workbook.
- Compare them with those on the completed checklist (page 110).
- Make any changes.

EXERCISE 3.27

- Add your new words and phrases to the style and tone section of the checklist.
- Rewrite your letter. Compare your letter with the example below.

Dear Mr Strauss

I wish to reserve display space and accommodation for the Summer Furniture Exhibition.

This year we require 5 display areas. We intend to use 3 of these for a display of living areas and 2 for bedrooms. We also need an office area for 3 people to work in and the services of a lighting technician. In addition, will you please reserve accommodation for 2 people for 2 nights?

As you know, we attended last year's exhibition and found it most enjoyable. We took several orders at the exhibition and a few more afterwards. We are looking for more new customers and more orders from German firms this year.

Please invoice our Accounts Department for the costs of all our reservations.

I look forward to your early confirmation of our booking.

Yours sincerely

Figure 3.10 Letter, situation/task 2: additional details and additional invented details

3.9.2 Improving style and tone in letters 3 to 10

You have now written letters for situations 1 and 2.

Compare your own letters with the letters in the Resources section on pages 123–4.

Do your letters work as well as the letters in the Resources section?

Remember: minor differences are not important.

KEYNOTES

Style and tone:

- Depend on the subject matter of the letter.
- Depend on the writer/addressee relationship.
- Depend on the purpose of the letter.
- Help the letter to do its job successfully.

3.10 Quality factor

After carefully studying this section you should be able to write a letter that will achieve a Credit (over 60%) or a Distinction (over 75%) on Examination Question 1.

This section continues the process of writing business letters as outlined in the Extended Syllabus topics 1.3.1 and 1.3.2.

3.10.1 Introduction and review

You have shown that you can now write a business letter that will achieve a Pass grade in English for Business First Level. You have 10 completed letters, plus your checklists and build-up sheets to prove this. You have developed many skills and you can be proud of the work you have done and the skills you have learned. But why stop here?

The title of this book is 'How to Pass English for Business First Level'. But at LCCIEB we want you to do better than a Pass. We want you to achieve a Credit or a Distinction.

At this stage some of the completed letters in the Resources section are a little short of the required 150 to 200 words called for in the Extended Syllabus. If these letters were written in the examination, a few marks would be lost because the letter is short. You will need to increase the length of letters to avoid losing marks. This is not a problem. The quality factor will do this for you.

The quality factor will help you to achieve a higher grade. Everything you have done so far in letter-writing has been a step by step process. The quality factor is just one more step in the process that you can easily learn and apply to your work.

What do we mean by 'the quality factor'?

It is really a matter of how you see the task of writing a business letter. Remember the original definition of a business letter:

> Definition
>
> A business letter is a formal written communication between an individual in one organisation and an individual in another organisation about a specific business matter, expressed simply and economically.

An adequate business letter:

- Orders some goods
- Asks about a product
- Informs a person about a conference
- Complains about poor service.

A good business letter also:

- Presents your firm as efficient
- Shows that you care about a customer
- Makes your customer feel special
- Promotes your products in the market.

To change an adequate business letter to a good business letter you need to think harder. You need to choose the words and phrases more carefully. You need to ask:

What do I really want this letter to achieve?

The rest of this chapter explores this idea.

We have agreed that a good business letter is a combination of 2 things:

1 A means of ordering, informing, complaining, congratulating, etc
2 An opportunity to promote a product, reassure a customer, demonstrate your efficiency, etc.

To achieve the second aspect you need to think about:

- How we regard a customer
- How we present our firm
- How we introduce a product
- How we write positively in the letter.

You must analyse the situation/task more closely by reading more carefully and thinking at a deeper level.

The quality factor steps extend the process you learned and applied in Section 3.9, Style and tone. The new information that you supplied using Section 3.9 was written in words and phrases. When you apply the quality factor you will be writing new sentences.

By following the quality factor steps, you will improve and lengthen the letter by adding more informative details to make the letter more persuasive.

EXERCISE 3.28

Adding the quality factor to Letter 1

Read carefully Version 4 of Letter 1 (Figure 3.8) (page 44).

Make a list in your workbook of 4 items that need more detail. Check your list against the following:

1 Roland Jenks
2 Venue
3 Games
4 Business outcome.

Write a sentence about each item that will make the letter more persuasive.

Check your list against the following:

1 I know you are especially interested in this market area.
2 The venue will be in our new conference suite.
3 We are very proud of both games; the technology is amazing.
4 I feel certain that both our companies will profit from this presentation.

The purpose of each of the new sentences is to:

1 tell Mr Jenks that you are interested in him as a person
2 assure him that the venue will be comfortable
3 present your opinion of the new games
4 indicate that the future will be profitable.

Here is the letter (now Version 5, the final version) with the new persuasive sentences added in **bold** (Figure 3.11).

Dear Mr Jenks

As one of our most valued customers, I am writing to invite you to the presentation of our latest computer business games. **I know you are especially interested in this area of the market.**

For special customers like yourself we are holding a half-day demonstration of our new games, 'Takeover' and 'Marketing Manager'. This important occasion will be on the morning of 26 March, starting at 10.00 am. **The venue will be our new conference centre.** Our Chief Designer, Ms Pauline Davi, will open the demonstration.

The timetable for the morning is as follows:

10.00 am   Arrival and coffee.

10.30 am   Introduction to new games by Ms Davi.

11.00 am   'Hands-on' session and questions.

12.00 pm   Buffet lunch.

'Takeover' is a game which presents the player with the problems of taking over another company. 'Marketing Manager' involves the player in methods for success in marketing and positive team building. **We are very proud of both games; the technology is amazing.** I am sure you will learn a lot from both games and find them, at the same time, very enjoyable.

I feel certain that our companies will profit from this presentation.

I look forward to the pleasure of seeing you at the demonstration.

Yours sincerely

Figure 3.11 Letter, situation/task 1: quality factor added

Note: Length approximately 195 words

As you followed the quality factor steps, you were reading more carefully and thinking more deeply about the information in the situation/task.

Remember that doing the exercises in Chapter 8, Language competence, on a regular basis will help you to write clear and accurate sentences. Although Chapter 8 does not deal with a specific examination question, your understanding of the information is crucial to success in the four examination questions, particularly Question 1, Letters and memos.

EXERCISE 3.29

Improving letter 2

Apply the quality factor process to Letter 2:

- Read situation/task carefully
- Read Letter 2, Version 4 carefully (page 45)
- Write in your workbook sentences which will:
  1 Add to the information about your company
  2 Add to the information about the furniture exhibition

Dear Mr Strauss

I wish to reserve space and accommodation for the summer exhibition.

Our company is expanding its range of products. This year we require 5 display areas. We intend to use 3 of these for a display of living areas and 2 for bedrooms. We also need an office area for 3 people to work in, and the services of a lighting technician. In addition, will you please reserve accommodation for 2 people for 2 nights?

As you know we attended last year's exhibition and found it most enjoyable. **The organisation of the exhibition last year was very good.** We took several orders at the exhibition and a few more afterwards. We are looking for more customers and more orders from German firms this year. **Our aim is to sell to every country in Europe by the year 2003.**

Please invoice our Accounts Department direct for the costs of our reservations.

Our MD sends you his best wishes.

I look forward to your early confirmation of our booking.

Yours sincerely

Nancy Lorimer

Nancy Lorimer

Assistant Manager

Figure 3.12 Letter, situation/task 2: quality factor added

Note: Length approximately 170 words

3 Present a positive image of your company

4 Make the addressee feel valued.

Compare your sentences with the following:

1 Our company is expanding its range of products.

2 The organisation of the exhibition last year was very good.

3 Our aim is to sell to every country in Europe by the year 2003.

4 Our Managing Director sends you his best wishes.

EXERCISE 3.30

Improving Letters 3 to 10

Follow the same procedure as in Exercise 3.29 to complete letters 3 to 10.

Remember:

Make sure that the new sentences

- Are relevant
- Make the letter more effective
- Use correct grammar and spelling.

When you have finished your final version of each letter, compare it with the completed letters. Check to see if there are places where you could improve your letter.

You have now completed the chapter on writing business letters.

Chapter 4 deals with how to write business memos. You will apply much of what you have learnt in Chapter 3 about letter-writing to memo-writing.

If there is something you still do not fully understand in this chapter, read the appropriate section again and re-do the exercises. Do not start the memo section until you are happy with everything in the letter-writing section.

KEYNOTES

The quality factor:

- Helps you to reach the higher grades in the examination.
- Gives your letter added interest for the reader.
- Shows how you value a customer.
- Shows how you present your company.
- Shows how you introduce your products.
- Shows how you write positively about the main subject matter.
- Makes your letter an opportunity to achieve an effect beyond simple communication.

POINTS TO REMEMBER

- **A business letter** is a formal written communication between the representatives of two organisations about a specific business matter.
- A business letter adopts a formal approach to layout and communication.
- A business letter keeps to the purpose.
- A business letter contains no irrelevant information.
- **The correct order for an address** is: name of person, number and street, town or city, postcode (zipcode), country.
- The writer's address is the address of the person writing the letter.
- The inside address is the address of the person receiving the letter.
- The writer's address is placed above the date.
- The writer's address never starts with a person's name.
- The writer's address always starts with the name of a company or a department.
- The inside address is placed below the date.
- The inside address always starts with the name or position of the person receiving the letter.
- It is now accepted practice NOT to use punctuation throughout the layout of a business letter. This practice is recommended by LCCIEB.
- **The salutation** is the correct term for saying 'hello' in a business letter.
- **The complimentary close** is the correct term for saying 'goodbye' in a business letter.
- If you know the name of the person, you write 'Dear Mr Smith . . . Yours sincerely'.
- If you do not know the name, you write 'Dear Sir (or Dear Madam) . . . Yours faithfully'.
- If you do not know the person's sex, you write 'Dear Sir or Madam . . . Yours faithfully'. (Note: this will not occur in EFB First Level.)
- If you do not know if a female is married or not, you write 'Dear Ms Smith . . . Yours sincerely'.
- You must never write the full name of the person (e.g. Dear John Smith).
- **Read the situation/task very carefully.**
- Decide what the letter is really about.
- Use coloured pens to underline the important points and make a list of these.
- Decide which point is the most important; all other points depend on this one.
- **The main subject matter** is the *core* of the letter.
- The main subject matter helps you to plan and put the letter in logical order.
- The main subject matter helps you to invent appropriate and relevant details of your own.
- **The key points** are the most important points in the letter.
- Underline the key points in the situation/task.
- Write the key points as a list.
- Key points do not include the writer's or the inside names or addresses.
- Write out the key points in 2 or 3 short sentences; this gives you the basic letter.
- **Additional details** are the minor points in the situation/task.
  - Write these down as a list.
  - Add these to your basic letter.
- **Additional invented details** are the details that you supply.
- Additional invented details are always relevant to the situation/task.

- Additional invented details 'add' to the content of your letter.
- You can add these to the existing letter.
- **The opening sentence** should
- Be relevant to the situation/task.
- Depend on who the letter is written to.
- Depend on the purpose of the letter.
- Introduce the main subject matter.
- Reflect the writer/addressee relationship.
- Be polite and business-like.
- Be fairly short.
- **The closing sentence** should
  - Be quite short.
  - Be polite and business-like.
  - Leave the reader of the letter 'satisfied'.
  - Have a purpose (saying goodbye, indicating future contact, etc).
  - NOT contain important information.
- **Style and tone**
  - Depend on the subject matter of the letter.
  - Depend on the writer/addressee relationship.
  - Depend on the purpose of the letter.
  - Help the letter to 'do its job' successfully.
- **The quality factor**
  - Helps you to reach the higher grades in the examination.
  - Gives your letter added interest for the reader.
  - Shows how you value a customer.
  - Shows how you present your company.
  - Shows how you introduce your products.
  - Shows how you write positively about the main subject matter.
  - Makes your letter an *opportunity* to achieve an effect beyond simple communication.

4

Memos

After studying this chapter and completing the exercises, the candidate should be able to:

1 *compose a memo using the information given in the examination question;*

2 *adopt an appropriate style or tone;*

3 *use the conventions for layout, language and paragraphing;*

4 *display coherence and cohesion to ensure fluent reading of the memo;*

5 *avoid over-use and unnecessary copying from the situation/task;*

6 *ensure that the memo is the right length for the stated purpose.*

Extended Syllabus references

1.1   Compose a memo on the basis of given data with a particular aim or instruction

1.2   Adopt an appropriate style or tone for the particular purpose

1.3   Employ consistent memo conventions regarding

    1.3.1   Layout

    1.3.2   Conventions of memo language

    1.3.3   Paragraphing

1.4   Display coherence and cohesion to ensure fluent reading of the memo

1.5   Avoid over-use and unnecessary copying from the information given

1.6   Ensure that the length of the memo is adequate for the stated purpose

1.7   Ensure that the finished memo is sendable

Definition

A memo is a formal written communication between staff members of the same organisation. A letter is between the representatives of two organisations. Another way of saying this is that:

- a memo is an internal communication (within an organisation)
- a letter is an external communication (between two organisations).

You will use the skills you learned in Chapter 3, Business letters, in doing the tasks in this chapter.

Main features of a memo are the same as those for a business letter:

- layout is conventional
- topic is specific
- content relates only to that topic
- style is simple and straightforward.

Examination Question 1 will ask you to write either a memo or a letter. You will not be asked to write both. Question 1 is worth 30 marks.

Layout	5
Content	15
Style/Tone	4
Accuracy of grammar and spelling	6

Memos:

- are sharply focused on a single topic
- use simple direct language
- use a logical format.

The main difference between a letter and a memo is the standard layout. Since a memo is a communication between two people in the same organisation, you do not need the detailed writer's address and inside address. The salutation, complimentary close and signature are not used.

Note: memo may be initialled.

There are 6 elements in the standard layout (Figure 4.1):

1   heading: Memo or Memorandum
2   To

    name of person you are sending the memo to → John Smith

    position held by person you are sending the memo to → Director of Purchasing

    a staff group → All truck drivers

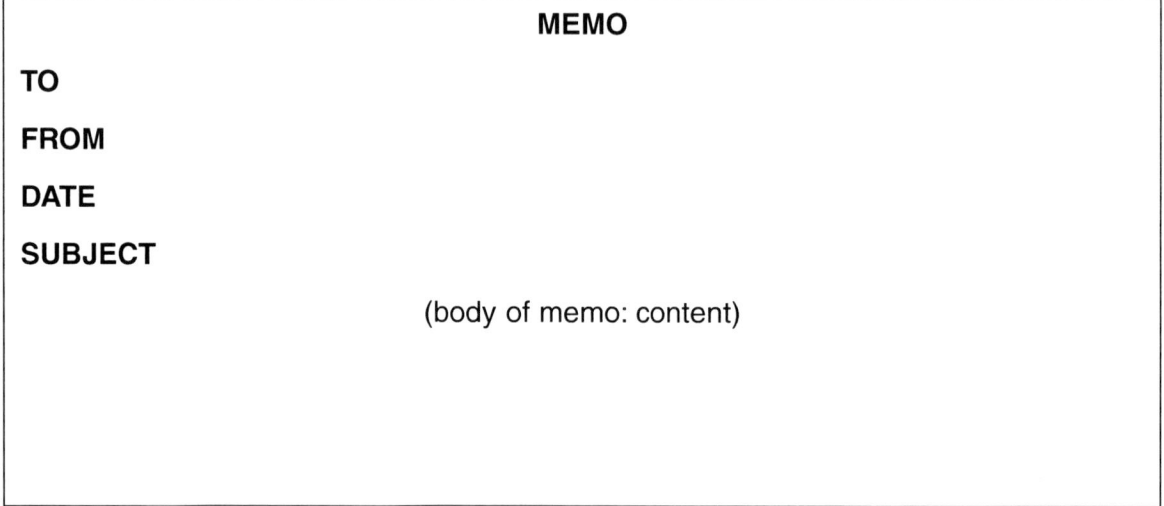

Figure 4.1   Memo, standard layout

3 From

In the exercises and the Examination Question, use your own name

4 Date

In the exercises and the Examination Question, use today's date

5 Subject

The reason you are writing the memo stated in a short phrase, not a sentence, eg:

− Traffic accidents

− New health insurance plan

6 Content

Follows the same pattern as the business letter (but no salutation or complimentary close)

− Opening sentence

− Content

− Closing sentence

− May be initialled (no signature).

Before you attempt the following exercises, make sure you have made 10 copies of the blank checklist on page 146 in the Resources section.

When you check your work against each completed checklist, look at only those parts of the checklists that are relevant for the exercise. Cover the rest of the checklist with a sheet of paper. It is important that you produce your own answers to the exercises before reading the answers in the completed checklists.

EXERCISE 4.1 COMPLETE MEMO 1

As you finish each item, compare it with the completed checklist. Make any changes to your work that you think will improve your memo.

Write the items in your blank checklist.

REMEMBER TO USE THE INFORMATION IN THE SECTIONS IN CHAPTER 3.

1 Read the situation/task carefully and underline the:

• Addressee

• Writer

• Subject.

You should have underlined:

Addressee: new Managing Director Bentham Ceramics/Eric Roberts

Writer: personal secretary (use your own name)

Subject: Carol Dando/to retire/evening party

To: Mr Eric Roberts

From: Student name

Date: Date of examination

Subject: Carol Dando's retirement party

2 Underline:

- key points (Section 3.6)
- additional details (Section 3.7).

3 Make a list of additional invented details (Section 3.8).

Arrange the key points, additional details and additional invented details in logical order.

4 Write an opening and a closing sentence (Section 3.8).

5 Create words and phrases to improve style and tone (Section 3.9).

6 Write sentences to apply the quality factor (Section 3.10).

Use your checklist to write a draft of the memo in your workbook.

Follow the general pattern:

- opening sentence
- paragraph 1
- paragraph 2
- paragraph 3
- closing sentence.

Compare your draft with the completed memo.

Make any changes you think are necessary.

Write the memo using the standard layout (Figure 4.1).

EXERCISE 4.2 COMPLETE MEMOS 2 TO 10

Follow the steps you used to write Memo 1.

You have now completed the chapter on memos.

Remember, Examination Question 1 will ask you to write either a letter or a memo.

You will not be asked to write both.

KEYNOTES

Compared to a letter, a memo is:

- More sharply focused on a single business-related topic.
- Simpler and more direct in its use of language.
- Totally business-like in style and tone.
- Simply and logically arranged.

5

Basic reading comprehension: true-or-false questions

After studying this chapter, you should be able to:

1 *read and understand a passage of about 300 words;*

2 *after reading 10 statements based on the passage, decide which statements are true and which are false;*

3 *copy the words from the passage that support your decision.*

Extended Syllabus references

2.1 Demonstrate an ability to read and understand a passage

2.2 Use the information in a passage to determine the validity of a series of statements

2.3 Select appropriate and brief information from the passage to support your opinions about the statements

2.4 Transfer accurately to the answer paper all words selected from the passage

2.5 Avoid the inclusion of all unnecessary words in the answers

5.1 Introduction

Examination Question 2 is based on this chapter. It is worth 30 marks.

- Correct answer, true or false   10 marks
- Correct choice of support statement   20 marks

The instructions at the beginning of the question are always the same:

- Read the passage (usually about 300 words).
- Mark each of the 10 statements true or false.
- Write down the exact words from the passage that support your choice.
- Do not copy more than 6 words for each answer.
- You will lose marks for copying unnecessary information.

Always:

- Read the passage carefully.
- Read the first statement, then re-read the passage until you find the evidence on which to decide whether the statement is true or false.
- Underline the words.
- Write down true or false.
- Copy the words (maximum 6) which support your answer.
- Check to make sure that you have copied the words accurately with no spelling mistakes.
- Repeat process for each of the statements.

5.2 Exercises

EXERCISE 5.1

Example

Sentence: In our office all the employees must be able to do several jobs

Statement: *The people who work with us do not have more than one skill.*

The statement is false, since the phrase in the sentence

- 'must be able to do several jobs'

implies that employees must have more than one skill, while the statement says they

- *do not have more than one skill.*

Now you know how to do this, try the 10 questions. Write the answers in your workbook. Check your answers when you have finished the exercise. You will find the answers for all the true/false exercises on pages 185–7.

1	Sentence:	In my company all employees have a maximum of 3 weeks holiday every year.
	True or false statement:	*Each year all my workers enjoy more than 3 weeks holiday.*
2	Sentence:	Ford cars have sales outlets all over the world.
	True or false statement:	*If you want a Ford car, you must travel to the USA.*
3	Sentence:	The rules in our firm state that private phone calls are not allowed.
	True or false statement:	*It is forbidden to telephone your family from our offices.*
4	Sentence:	All our employees receive a bonus twice a year.
	True or false statement:	*There is an annual bonus for our employees.*
5	Sentence:	In the clothing industry there are as many female managers as male managers.
	True or false statement:	*The clothing industry employs more males than females as managers.*
6	Sentence:	Last year bus fares rose by no more than 2%.
	True or false statement:	*Last year there was a huge increase in bus fares.*
7	Sentence:	I always check my e-mail at the start of the day.
	True or false statement:	*Most days I leave checking my e-mail until lunchtime.*
8	Sentence:	We insist on a reply before the end of the month.
	True or false statement:	*An immediate response is necessary.*

9 Sentence: The goods you ordered will be delivered in 5 to 6 days.
   True or false statement: *It will be almost a week before you receive the goods.*

10 Sentence: We run a spell check on all letters to foreign customers.
   True or false statement: *Most of our letters to foreign addresses are spell checked.*

EXERCISE 5.2

Read the passage about oil prices.

Say whether each statement is **true** or **false**.

Tick the phrase you would quote from the text to support your answer precisely and in the fewest number of words.

The rising price of oil

Are we heading for the next oil crisis? Oil prices are rising fast – soon the price of petrol for the UK motorist will be £4 a gallon – and are a big threat to the world economy. The price of crude oil in 1992 was about $10 a barrel; now it is $30 a barrel. This is because less oil is produced. Last year OPEC (Organisation of Petroleum Exporting Countries) cut production. Other sources of oil in the world are running out. The OPEC countries will meet soon in Vienna to decide how much oil they will produce in the next 2 years. The US wants them to produce 2 million barrels a day, but they may only produce 1 million barrels. That means the West will be short of oil.

---

1 World oil prices are slowly increasing.
   True/False
   (a) petrol £4 a gallon
   (b) rising fast
   (c) sources running out

2 Since 1992 the cost of a barrel of oil has more than doubled.
   True/False
   (a) 2 million barrels a day
   (b) was about $10...now $30
   (c) less oil is produced

3 It will not be long before the OPEC countries hold a meeting.
   True/False
   (a) meet soon
   (b) decide how much
   (c) countries in the Middle East

4 Apart from the OPEC countries, there is plenty of oil in the world.
   True/False
   (a) other sources running out
   (b) US produces 2 million
   (c) West soon short of oil

5 The price of oil does not affect global trade.
   True/False
   (a) big threat to world economy
   (b) less oil is produced
   (c) heading for next oil crisis.

Answers are on page 185.

EXERCISE 5.3

Read carefully the passage entitled 'E-mail'. Say whether the following statements are **true** or **false**. Copy the words or phrase which support your answer. Do not write more than 6 words for each answer. You will lose marks for irrelevant information.

Write your answers on the lines marked A.

1 Letters sent by normal post always arrive on the same day.

A _____

2 Exchanging letters by normal post is faster than by e-mail.

A _____

3 With e-mail you have to write your own address every time you send a message.

A _____

4 You listen to e-mails on your telephone handset.

A _____

5 E-mail is proving to be very expensive for businesses.

A _____

6 It is more complicated to reply to an e-mail than to send one.

A _____

7 You 'post' an e-mail by dialling on your telephone.

A _____

8 There is no limit on earth to where you can send an e-mail.

A _____

9 Your e-mail message can be more than a single sheet of paper.

A _____

10 Businesses use e-mail very little today.

A _____

Check your answers before you start the next exercise. The correct answers are on page 186.

E-mail

What is this new thing called e-mail? E-mail simply stands for 'electronic mail'. It is a method of sending letters and other information from one person to another.

To send ordinary mail you need certain tools, such as a pen, paper, envelope and a stamp; you also need tools to send e-mails – a computer, a modem, and access to an e-mail service provider.

To begin with think how a handwritten letter is sent to another person. With such a letter the writer puts his/her address at the top of the first page, writes the letter and then signs it. The letter is then placed in an envelope, the address of the person it is going to is written on the envelope, a stamp is attached and the letter goes into the post box. The letter is usually delivered a day or two later and the person it is sent to replies in the same way. This process takes up a lot of time.

E-mail works in a similar way, but in this case you tell the computer your address just once, and it remembers it for future occasions. You write the body of the letter, sign it if you wish, and add the address it is going to. 'Posting' the letter needs only a single click on your 'mouse' or a single stroke on your keyboard. The letter, or 'message' in e-mail language, then goes via your telephone line to another computer (which can be anywhere in the world). The computer stores the message until the person it is going to reads it. The same process is used for the reply. Using e-mail, a message can be sent anywhere in the world almost in an instant. This may not matter when you send a friendly letter about your family, but in the business world e-mail is a big saver of time and money. Whole documents can be sent from one person to another by e-mail. This helps people to work faster and to get in touch much more quickly. As businesses use e-mail more and more, the need to respond more quickly can make life very stressful. It may be the price we have to pay for instant communication.

Source   Adapted from 'Introducing the Internet', *Guardian,* February 2000.

EXERCISE 5.4

Read carefully the passage entitled 'Why do we use so much paper?'. Say whether the following statements are **true** or **false**. Copy the words or phrase that support your answer. Do not write more than 6 words for each answer. You will lose marks for irrelevant information.

Write your answers on the lines marked A.

1   Offices are not reducing the amount of paper they use.

    A _____

2   It is not necessary to keep copies of the letters we send.

    A _____

3   As technology develops, we use paper less and less.

    A _____

4   Computers are the safest way of storing information.

    A _____

5   World-wide use of paper is less than 28 million tonnes a year.

    A _____

6   Computers have been used by businesses for less than 50 years.

    A _____

7   About 50% of the total goods sold are sold without packaging.

    A _____

8   Telephone bills take only a single sheet of paper.

    A _____

9   Credit card systems do not use any paper at all.

    A _____

10 Around 50% of our daily post is sent by strangers.

    A _____

Check your answers before you start the next exercise. The correct answers are on page 186.

Why do we use so much paper?

We have had computers in offices and most other places of work for about 20 years. People thought that, as we used computers more, we would use less paper. We do not need to print on paper many of the business letters and documents which we send to companies. We can send them from one computer to another by e-mail. We do not need to keep paper copies of letters because we have already stored them on computer disks. We can even find all sorts of information (useful in our commercial and private lives) on the Internet and on CD ROM. So, once more, we can read it on the computer screen rather than from a sheet of paper.

People who predicted that we would use less paper were totally wrong. Offices, in fact, use 6% more paper each year. In Western Europe alone, in every 12 months, the business world uses over 30 million tonnes of printing and writing paper. Before the computer became an essential piece of office equipment, we used only a third of that amount.

There is generally more paper in our lives now than in the 1980s and 1990s. Almost everything we buy is packed using paper. Half of our private mail is junk mail from people we do not know who either want to sell us books, holidays and insurance, or to offer us credit cards or bank loans. Newspapers are bigger than ever with business, sport, television and arts supplements which not everybody wants. In some countries every house has 2 or 3 weekly free newspapers which are full of advertisements.

New technology, inside and outside offices, makes us use more paper too. We print copies readily and easily from our computers. Every time we use debit or credit cards we have paper receipts, then paper bills and statements at least every month. Office workers use fax machines and photocopiers every hour of their lives. As technology makes it easy for telephone companies to list every call we make, the telephone bill for every small company is several pages long.

▶

Why, then, can we not do without paper? It is simply because it reassures us that our information is safe. Things go wrong with computers and data can get lost. But if we have a copy on paper, we have a permanent record of our business dealings.

EXERCISE 5.5

Read carefully the passage 'The Suez Canal in Egypt'. Say whether the following statements are **true** or **false**. Copy the words or phrase that support your answer. Do not write more than 6 words for each answer. You will lose marks for irrelevant information.

Write your answers on the lines marked A.

1   The Suez Canal took 10 years to build.

A _____

2   At first the canal was largely built by foreigners using the latest technology.

A _____

3   In 1865 ships could go through the canal at night.

A _____

4   Tourist use of the canal is increasing every year.

A _____

5   All of the canal is now wide enough for 2 ships to pass.

A _____

6   In 1876 the sole owner of the canal was the Egyptian government.

A _____

7   Several countries provided the money to build the canal.

A _____

8   Going through the canal was a slow and dangerous journey.

A _____

9   It took more people to build the canal than it takes to operate it today.

A _____

10   There are more passenger ships using the canal than any other type.

A _____

Check your answers before you start the next exercise. The correct answers are on page 186.

The Suez Canal in Egypt

The Suez Canal was built between 1859 and 1869 to give ships a short route from the Mediterranean Sea to the Red Sea.

At first 25,000 Egyptian workers did much of the work without machines. It was hard work. The men lived in poor, unhealthy conditions, and hundreds died. Later they used machines, and European workers helped too.

The canal cost 433 million French francs to build – twice as much as the canal company expected. Most of the money came from French investors. The rest came from the Egyptian government. People were worried that, because it cost so much to build, it would never make a profit.

In fact, it was so popular that in 1875, the British government bought the Egyptian government's shares and became the principal shareholder. The reasons for its popularity were that it was safe and quick. At first ships could only use the canal by day. By 1875 some ships had huge electric lights, and they could use the canal safely at night.

Today the Egyptian government owns the canal, and earns 2 billion dollars a year from it. To operate the canal there are 20,000 employees. The canal is 4 times wider than it was when it was built and along half of the canal ships can pass going in opposite directions.

Most of the ships which now use the canal carry cargo (30 million tonnes a year). 50 years ago a million tourists used the canal, but now there are very few. Tourists today travel by plane.

EXERCISE 5.6

Read carefully the passage entitled 'The Telephone in Business'. Say whether the following statements are **true** or **false**. Copy the words or phrase from the passage which support your answer. Do not write more than 6 words for each answer. You will lose marks for irrelevant information.

Write your answers on the lines marked A.

1 In 1916 telephone calls were connected by hand; now a machine is used.

   A _____

2 Many companies rely on the telephone for a lot of their business.

   A _____

3 Teleconferences are used frequently and are economical.

   A _____

4 Unlike public telephones mobile phones can be used absolutely anywhere.

   A _____

5 Many mobile phone calls are simply a waste of time.

   A _____

6 Public telephones only operate on land.

A _____

7 If you pay a bill by phone, you must first contact the company.

A _____

8 Telephones do not help bank profits.

A _____

9 Telephones have permanently changed the way people contact each other.

A _____

10 Mobile phones have been in existence for no more than 20 years.

A _____

Check your answers before you start the next exercise. The correct answers are on pages 186–7.

The Telephone in Business

When the first telephone call was made in 1876, it started a revolution and affected forever how we communicate with our friends and family, and how we do business.

The telephone's great advantage is speed. Usually it takes only a few seconds to contact anyone in any part of the world. Over 50 years ago it took longer because every call had to be connected manually by an operator. Now it is done automatically and we use an operator only when we have difficulty in placing a call.

The telephone means that we can do business instantly. Many companies today depend on the telephone for much of their business. To book a seat at the cinema or on a train, the majority of customers use the telephone. To arrange insurance or a holiday, companies encourage their customers to use the telephone. They can even pay by telephone, simply by giving the number of their credit or debit card. Written communication, by letter, comes second and often only confirms the arrangement already made by phone.

Some companies only do business by telephone. Banks, for example, save a lot of money if they do not have offices in every town. Customers can get their cash from a machine, and for other things they use the postal service or a courier, or they rely solely on telephone banking.

In the business world teleconferences have become quite common. Instead of travelling long distances to talk to each other, several people in different parts of the country or even the world can hold a conference over the telephone and so save time and money. The time it saves allows business people to deal with more customers.

Public telephones are everywhere in our towns, on street corners, in cafés or at rail stations. Even while travelling by plane, boat or train, we can use a public telephone.

The mobile phone (invented as long ago as 1976) is even more convenient. No matter where we are, we can keep in touch with our company – even while we are walking down the street. But many people misuse mobile phones when they receive a call from a colleague or a customer whilst travelling home by public transport. A lot of these calls are completely unnecessary; they just make these people feel important.

EXERCISE 5.7

Read carefully the passage entitled 'A Fishy Business'. Say whether the following statements are **true** or **false**. Copy the words or phrase from the passage that support your answer. Do not write more than 6 words for each answer. You will lose marks for irrelevant information.

Write your answers on the lines marked A.

1 Fish has only one use – as a source of food for human beings.

A _____

2 There is much less fish in the sea than a few years ago.

A _____

3 'Farming' fish means catching as much fish as you can.

A _____

4 Overfishing is the only cause of the declining numbers of fish.

A _____

5 Governments now regulate the times and the amounts of fish that can be caught.

A _____

6 It is estimated that there are 200 million fishermen in the world.

A _____

7 Factory ships go to sea for short periods and bring back fresh fish.

A _____

8 More than a third of Iceland's total income comes from selling fish to its people.

A _____

9 50% of the people in the world live in coastal areas.

A _____

10 Raising fish prices is no help to the fisherman, because sales volume drops.

A _____

Check your answers carefully. The correct answers are on page 187.

A Fishy Business

The sea covers 71% of the earth's surface. Half the people in the world live less than 100 km from the sea. There are probably 12.5 million fishermen in the world taking fish from the sea, and the fish they catch are not only for people to eat. To the business world the sea, and what is in it, is extremely important. We use oil from fish to make margarine and even paint. Many pet foods are partly made from fish.

200 million people depend on the fishing industry for jobs – building ships, repairing ships, processing fish in factories, and transporting and selling products which are made entirely or partly from fish. So it is a big and important industry.

It is particularly important for some countries. Iceland, for example, earns 30% of its income from exporting fish.

Modern ways of fishing are very efficient but also very expensive. Companies buy massive factory ships in which the fish are cleaned, prepared for sale and frozen. To make a profit the ships need to be in use most of the time and to handle huge numbers of fish. Ships are often at sea for several weeks at a time.

The problem is that there are not enough fish in the sea and the numbers are declining because some people catch too many, and other people pollute the sea which kills some of the fish.

Governments are trying to solve the problem by paying some fishermen to leave the industry and do other jobs. They also tell fishermen how many days they can work, how many fish they can catch each year, and how big those fish should be. This often causes arguments. The fishermen say that if they cannot fish all the time, they cannot earn enough money to live on.

A new idea is to increase the price of fish so much that fishermen need to catch and sell fewer fish to make a living. In that way, perhaps there will be some fish left in the sea for the future. But consumers also have a viewpoint. If fish is too expensive, they do not buy it. This causes hardship to the fish seller and the fishermen.

The best way to improve fish stocks is to 'farm' the fish. This means breeding and feeding fish at sea under controlled conditions. This is done in a closed area, so that the fish cannot escape into the open sea.

KEYNOTES

- Read all the information at least once.
- State 'true' or 'false' for each of the 10 statements. If you miss this out, you cannot score any marks.
- Write support material for every answer.
- Write no more than 6 support words for each answer. If you write more, you will lose marks.
- Support words must be copied directly from the passage. Do not use your own words.
- Support words may come from different parts of the passage.

6

Information processing: short-answer questions

After completing this chapter, you should be able to:

1 *read and understand a table or chart;*

2 *answer simple questions based on the data given.*

Extended Syllabus references

3.1 Read and understand a table or chart

3.2 Compare the information in order to answer simple questions based on the data contained in a table or chart

3.3 Answer using a single word or figure

3.4 Avoid use of all unnecessary information

6.1 Introduction

Examination Question 3 is based on this chapter. It is worth 20 marks. Questions are based on information given in a chart or table.

About charts:

(Examples are taken from the chart in Exercise 6.4, page 73.)

- Every chart has a title.
  Cookery Titles In Stock

- Charts consist of a series of columns separated by vertical lines. Each column has a heading.
  Title, Author, Price, Year published, etc

- Horizontal lines create cells. Each cell contains one piece of information.
  Mediterranean Food: a title
  E. David: a name
  24.99: a price
  1995: a year
  H: a letter
  270: a number

Read the question carefully and underline the column you should look in.

1 How many books are available in <u>paperback</u>?

You will need to look in the column Hardback (H)/Paperback (P).

To answer some questions you will need to look in two or three columns.

16   Which book with less than <u>100</u> <u>colour</u> <u>illustrations</u> <u>costs</u> the most?

The two columns are Number of Colour Illustrations, Price.

Steps to follow to answer a question:

- Read the column headings carefully
- Read the question carefully
- Underline the information you need
- Decide which column contains the information
- Identify the cell with the information you need
- Copy the information exactly.

More complicated questions will require that you select more than one column.

10   Was '<u>Mediterranean Food</u>' <u>published</u> before <u>M. Hagan's</u> book?

Mediterranean Food: title column
Published: published column
M. Hagan: author column

You will need to compare the year Mediterranean Food was published – 1995, with the year M. Hagan's book was published – 1989, to decide which was published first.

If you mark each piece of information you are going to need with a highlighter pen as you find it, it will be easier for you to make the calculations needed to answer the question.

Markers

Markers are used to indicate that there are exceptions to the information. The meaning of the marker is given in a footnote. Markers can be:

- Asterisks *
- Double asterisks **
- Hache marks #

Look at Exercise 6.3, pages 71–2.

The service operates daily from 08.00 till 18.00**

Footnote reads:
Sundays till 13.00 only from 1 January to 1 April.

You will need this information to answer questions such as:

5   What time does the last bus leave Keswick on Sunday January 19?

Markers also are used in individual cells. See Exercise 6.7, page 76.

Each question has four parts:

1 situation
2 task
3 chart or table
4 questions

Question 3 is the most straightforward of the examination questions. Always use the following steps:

- read the situation carefully
- the task is always worded in the same way, as follows:

Task

Study the chart carefully, then answer the questions that follow. Write your answer as a single word or a name, or as a number. Do not write more than this. You will lose marks for unnecessary information.

- Read the headings of each column
- Read the question carefully
- Underline the words that correspond to the column headings
- Find the cell in each column that provides the information you need
- Copy the information exactly as it appears in the cell
- Note: for some questions you will need to use more than one column
- Check the answers (pages 187–90)
- If your answer is wrong, work backwards from the correct answer to find out where you made your mistake.

6.2 Exercises

EXERCISE 6.1

Situation: You work in the despatch department of Wines by Post. You have been asked to check some facts about the latest offers of wine.

Task: Study the chart entitled 'Wines of the World', then answer the questions that follow. Write your answer as a single word, a name, or a number. You will lose marks for unnecessary information.

WINES OF THE WORLD

Wine name	Country	Year	Price £	Grape	Colour
Santenay	France	1998	5.00	Merlot	Red
Soave	Italy	1999	6.00	Garganega	White
Maipo Valley	Chile	1995	8.00	Merlot	Red
Rheingau	Germany	1998	4.50	Riesling	White
Cotnari	Romania	1996	3.50	Grasa	White
Penedes	Spain	1995	6.50	Tempranillo	Red

1 From which country does the cheapest red wine come?

2 How many white wines cost less than £5.00?

3 Santenay and Maipo Valley are from the same grape. Is this true?

4 Which is the oldest white wine in the list?

5 Is Garganega a region of Romania?

Check your answers before you do the next exercise.
The correct answers for this exercise are on page 187.

EXERCISE 6.2

Situation: You work in the tourist information office in your home city. You are checking the details about various local festivals.

Task: Study the chart below, then answer the questions that follow. Write your answer as a single word or name, or a number. You will lose marks for unnecessary information.

LOCAL FESTIVALS

Date	Festival	Venue	Number of days	Leader	Activities
6 April	Easter Flowers	Central Park	3	Mayor	Folk dancing
10 June	Summer Carnival	City centre	1	Mayor	Street processions
16 August	City Foundation	Sports arena	4	National president	Sports and concerts
22 December	Christmas	City centre	3	Mayor	Torchlight procession to cathedral

1 Which festival has dancing?

2 Which festival lasts the longest?

3 For how many festivals is the mayor the leader?

4 How many festivals are not in the city centre?

5 How many festivals have live music?

6 Is the Christmas festival longer than the Easter Flowers festival?

7 Which festival finishes on 19 August?

8 How many days of festivals are there altogether?

9 Central Park has 2 festivals. Is this true or false?

10 Who will lead the torchlight procession?

Check your answers before you start the next exercise.
The correct answers for this exercise are on page 187.

EXERCISE 6.3

Situation: Your company, Red Line Transport, whose head office is in Preston, is starting a new service in the north-west of the area. You have to check the timetable and fare details before it goes to the printer.

Task: Study the chart, then answer the questions that follow. Write your answer as a single word or name, or as a number. You will lose marks for unnecessary information.

KESWICK – WINDERMERE – KESWICK SERVICE

Buses leave every hour. This service operates daily from 08.00 till 18.00**
Journey takes $1\frac{1}{2}$ hours.
Bus capacity 60 persons.

Keswick								
£1.80	Naddle							
£3.60	£1.80	Dunmail						
£3.60	£3.60	£1.80	Thirlspot					
£3.60	£3.60	£3.60	£1.80	Grasmere				
£4.50	£4.50	£3.60	£3.60	£1.80	Rydal			
£4.50	£4.50	£4.50	£3.60	£3.60	£1.80	Ambleside		
£7.20	£4.50	£4.50	£3.60	£3.60	£3.60	£1.80	Waterhead	
£7.20	£7.20	£4.50	£4.50	£3.60	£3.60	£1.80	£1.80	Windermere

**Sundays till 13.00 only from 1 January to 1 April

Notes: The table shows the single adult fares.
         Children under 6 years old travel free with parents.
         Children under 14 years old half fare (not National Holidays).
         The return fare is twice the single fare.
         A family ticket is twice the adult fare.

1 What is the single fare from Keswick to Thirlspot?
2 Travelling from Keswick, what is the third stop?
3 What is the adult return fare from Dunmail to Rydal?
4 What is the cheapest return fare?
5 What time does the last bus leave Keswick on Sunday 19 January?
6 How often do the buses run?
7 Is the Rydal to Thirlspot fare the same as the fare from Dunmail to Rydal?
8 In which town is the company head office?
9 Can I travel from Rydal to Thirlspot after 14.00 on Sunday 2 February?
10 How many passengers can travel on a bus at the same time?
11 What is the single fare from Ambleside to Dunmail?
12 Starting from Waterhead, is the fare to Naddle the same as the fare to Keswick?
13 What is the full fare from Ambleside to Grasmere for a mother and her 4-year-old twins?
14 What is the name of the bus company?
15 How many stops are there on a return journey from Waterhead to Naddle?
16 Travelling to Keswick, what is the fourth stop after Rydal?
17 How many hours does the full return journey take?
18 On a National Holiday what is the fare for a 12 year old travelling with his mother from Keswick to Waterhead?
19 How many different single adult fares (prices) are there on the route?
20 How much is a single journey family ticket from Dunmail to Waterhead?

Check your answers before you start the next exercise.
The correct answers for this exercise are on pages 187–8.

EXERCISE 6.4

Situation: You work in the Sales Department of Rushmore Mail Order Books Ltd. You have been asked to check some items in the Cookery section.

Task: Study the chart below carefully, then answer the questions that follow. Write your answer as a single word or name, or as a number. Do not write more than this. You will lose marks for unnecessary information.

COOKERY TITLES IN STOCK

Title	Author	Price ($)US	Published	Hardback (H) Paperback (P)	Number of pages	Number of colour illustrations
Mediterranean Food	E. David	24.99	1995	H	270	100
Chinese Cookbook	P. Chapman	16.00	1997	H	200	150
Step by Step Thai Cookery	C. Bowen	24.99	2000	H	354	0
Indian Cooking	P. Lal	11.99	1997	P	259	200
Good Food from Morocco	P. Wolfen	9.95	2000	P	167	75
French Bistro Cookery	P. Laval	14.99	1994	H	225	130
Hot Wok Recipes	K. Hom	17.99	1999	H	300	200
Cooking in Vietnam	D. Sung	6.99	1993	P	137	65
Italian Cookery	M. Hagan	18.99	1989	H	342	225

1 How many books are available in paperback?

2 Which title has the most colour illustrations?

3 Which title has the smallest number of pages?

4 How many titles were published in 1997?

5 Who is the author of the cheapest hardback book?

6 How many paperbacks have less than 100 colour illustrations?

7 Is *Italian Cookery* cheaper than *Hot Wok Recipes*?

8 How many hardback books have more than 300 pages?

9 Whose book is the cheapest in the list?

10 Was *Mediterranean Food* published before M. Hagan's book?

11 How many hardback titles contain the word 'cookery'?

12 How much is the hardback with over 250 pages and the most colour illustrations?

13 How many books were published before 1998?

14 Which book published before 1996 costs the most?

15 In family name alphabetical order, which author is third?

16 Which book with less than 100 illustrations is the cheapest?

17 How many hardbacks published before 1997 have more than 250 pages?

18 Has K. Hom's book more colour illustrations than P. Lal's book?

19 How many books cost less than $US15.00?

20 How many hardback titles contain the word 'food'?

Check your answers before you start the next exercise.
The correct answers for this exercise are on page 188.

EXERCISE 6.5

Situation: You are planning to buy new carpet for all your offices.

Task: Study the chart below, then answer the questions that follow. Write your answer as a single word or name, or as a number. Do not write more than this. You will lose marks for unnecessary information.

Carpet name	Price per metre (£)	Grade	Guarantee (years)	Number of colours	Free fitting	Delivery time (days)
Axwell	35	A	10	20	Yes	7
Bartlett	30	B	5	10	No	3
Wilton	40	A	8	12	Yes**	14
Carvel	25	B	3	12	Yes	14
Fairfax	28	B	5	6	No	7
Sangster	45	A	10	14	No	21
Longton	38	A	10	14	Yes	14
McCain	24	B	4	8	Yes	10
Sheraton	32	A	6	24	Yes	10
Kendal	15	C	1	10	No	3

** for orders over 100 metres.

1 Which grade A carpet has the shortest delivery time?

2 How many grade B carpets cost less than £26 per metre?

3 Which grade B carpet has the shortest guarantee?

4 Is the delivery time for Fairfax the same as for Axwell?

5 Which grade A carpet has the largest colour choice?

6 Which is the most expensive carpet with a 10-year guarantee?

7 McCain has more colour choice than Fairfax. Is this true?

8 How many grade A carpets begin with the letter 'S'?

9 Which grade B carpet has free fitting and the lowest guarantee?

10 Which grade of carpet has free fitting and the longest delivery time?

11 Which grade B carpet has the least colours and no free fitting?

12 How many grade A carpets take longer than 12 days to deliver?

13 How many grade A and grade B carpets have free fitting for all orders?

14 Which is the cheapest grade B carpet with under 10 days' delivery?

15 Does Kendal have the shortest delivery time and the poorest guarantee?

16 Longton costs more than all other carpets with the same delivery time. Is this true?

17 What is the delivery time of the grade B carpet with the fewest colours?

18 How many grade A carpets have more colours than all the grade B carpets?

19 Which carpet with free fitting in grades A and B has the shortest guarantee?

20 How many carpets costing £30 or more have more than 10 colours?

Check your answers before you start the next exercise.
The correct answers for this exercise are on page 189.

EXERCISE 6.6

Situation: You are employed in your firm as Assistant Training Officer. You are looking at suitable business courses offered by a number of local colleges for business personnel. The chart below shows the courses at Kingston College in your area.

Task: Study the chart for Kingston College carefully, then answer the questions that follow. Write your answer as a single word or a name, or as a number. Do not write more than this. You will lose marks for unnecessary information.

KINGSTON COLLEGE (BUSINESS DEPARTMENT)

Course title	No of weeks	Level	Type	Course day	Cost (£)	Exam board	Enrolment fee (£)
Business Administration	30	Basic	Day	Tuesday	96	LCCIEB	10
Mail Merge 2	33	Advanced	Day	Thursday	85	OCR	5
Practice Management	33	Intermediate	Evening	Wednesday	194	AMSPAR	0
Text Processing	30	Advanced	Day/ evening	Tuesday	96	OCR	5
Supervisory Management	34	Intermediate	Evening	Thursday	194	NEBSM	20
Business Technology	16	Basic	Day	Tuesday	75	LCCIEB	10
Word Progression	20	Intermediate	Day	Monday	120	OCR	5
Personal Assistants	30	Advanced	Day/ evening	Wednesday	100	LCCIEB	10
Reception	20	Intermediate	Evening	Tuesday	90	LCCIEB	10
Retail Operations	30	Advanced	Day	Monday	150	LCCIEB	10

1 Which course has the highest enrolment fee?

2 How many courses are offered by LCCIEB?

3 Has OCR the least number of courses?

4 Which advanced course takes place on Thursday?

5 Which course costs the least?

6 Is Word Progression a longer course than Reception?

7 How many courses cost less than £85?

8   How many LCCIEB courses costing over £80 meet on Tuesday?

9   How many intermediate courses cost less than £100?

10   How many Wednesday courses have a £10 enrolment fee?

11   Which advanced OCR course runs both evening and daytime?

12   Which intermediate course runs the same day as Personal Assistants?

13   All OCR courses cost less than all LCCIEB courses. Is this true?

14   How many LCCIEB intermediate courses take place in the evening?

15   The cheapest advanced course is run by OCR. Is this true?

16   There are more day courses on Wednesday than on Tuesday. Is this true?

17   Do all advanced courses run for longer than all intermediate courses?

18   Does Practice Management cost the same as Supervisory Management?

19   Which basic course is as long as Text Processing?

20   Which LCCIEB course on Tuesday costs less than Mail Merge 2?

Check your answers before you start the next exercise.
The correct answers for this exercise are on page 189.

EXERCISE 6.7

Situation: Your company, Easytravel Ltd, is planning to offer a car hire service to customers. Your manager has asked you to prepare a report on the car hire charges of other firms. The charges for one firm, Columbus Rentacar Ltd, are shown in the table below.

Task: Study the table for Columbus Rentacar Ltd, then answer the questions that follow. Write your answer as a single word or name, or as a number. Do not write more than this. You will lose marks for unnecessary information.

COLUMBUS RENTACAR LTD
(Car rental costs per week)

Name	Group	Engine size (litres)	No of doors	Price April to July	Price August to October	km weekly limit	Child seat
Mercury	A	1.1	2	$150	$190	2,000*	No
Jupiter	B	1.6	4	$190	$220	No limit	No
Corniche#	C	2.0	4	$210	$230	2,000*	Yes
Maipo	D	2.5	4	$220	$270	No limit	Yes
Alandra	A	1.3	4	$170	$200	1,500	Yes
Larnaca	B	1.7	5	$185	$215	2,500	No
Panama**	D	2.3	5	$235	$260	No limit	No
Benidorm	A	1.4	5	$170	$190	1,500	No
Frejus	C	1.8	4	$200	$230	2,200*	Yes
Barbera	C	1.8	5	$220	$245	No limit	No

* excess charged at $5 per 1,000 km
** must be booked 3 days in advance
\# driver must be 21 or over

1   Which car has the smallest engine?

2   How many cars cost under $200 in May?

3   Has the Maipo more doors than the Barbera?

4   Which group C car has no weekly limit?

5   How many group A cars have a child seat?

6   Which car can a 19 year old not drive?

7   Which car has the biggest cost increase between July and August?

8   Do all group C cars have an engine size over 1.6 litres?

9   How many group B cars have no weekly limit?

10 Do all group D cars have more doors than the Larnaca?

11 How many 'no limit' cars have a child seat?

12 Which group C car costs the most in August?

13 How many 4-door cars have no weekly limit?

14 It is Monday. Which is the largest car with a child seat that I can drive today?

15 Which car has an engine size nearest to the Jupiter?

16 How many cars cost less than $220 at all times from April to October?

17 How many cars with an engine over 1.5 have only 4 doors and a child seat?

18 Which group has the most cars with no weekly limit?

19 It is 10 August. How much must I pay for a car with a child seat and no weekly limit?

20 It is September and I have $200. I need to travel 1200 km. Which car with more than 2 doors is the cheapest to rent?

Check your answers.
The correct answers for this exercise are on page 190.

KEYNOTES

- Read all the information carefully.
- Read and understand any footnotes; these can affect your answers.
- Write your answer as a single word, a name, or in figures.
- If the answer is a name, you are allowed to write the full name (e.g. John Smith or Fast Trak Computers).
- Check your answers carefully.

7

Text and data reformulation: forms and diagrams

After completing this chapter, you should be able to:

1 *read and understand information given in a situation;*

2 *select the items needed to complete a chart, form or list;*

3 *write briefly and accurately.*

Extended Syllabus references

4.1 Understand given material or data

4.2 Select from material to complete a chart or list

4.3 Use material to complete a business-related form (e.g. form for staffing rotas, accident report form, order or delivery form, chart showing a simple company staffing structure)

4.4 Use appropriate, precise and accurate wording

7.1 Introduction

Examination Question 4 is based on this chapter. It is worth 20 marks. The question is in the form of a situation/task.

Situation information is contained in one of the following forms:

- Written notes
- Conversation
- Telephone message
- Fax
- E-mail.

The task will be to complete items such as a:

- Form: an accident report form or a delivery form
- Chart: flight arrivals, company staffing structure or an interview timetable.

This is a straightforward assignment. You will be able to complete it successfully if you:

- Read the task (what you are being asked to do) carefully.
- Make a list of the information you need.
- Read the situation for each item on the list.
- Fill in the chart or form.

Example (Information will be found in Exercise 7.1)

1 List the information needed:
- Branch names
- Year of opening
- Names of managers
- Branches must be listed in order of opening.

2 Find the information. Underline the names of the branch offices. List them.
- Toronto
- Ho Chi Minh City
- Oslo
- Warsaw.

Note: London is the head office so it is not listed as a branch.

3 Write the opening date beside each branch name:
- Toronto   1999
- Ho Chi Minh City 1998 (1 year after Oslo)
- Oslo   1997 (2 years before Toronto)
- Warsaw   this year.

4 Arrange the branches in order of opening: Oslo, Ho Chi Minh City, Toronto, Warsaw.

5 Find the names of the managers for each city.

Oslo is easy. 'Oskar Gunnarsen is in charge of the Oslo office.'

The next sentence is confusing. 'The other 2 are managed by Hannah Samuels and Lee Cheng.' You don't know the specific city.

The next sentence is the clue. 'Lee is a native of Ho Chi Minh, so he fits in very well there.'

This means that Hannah must be the Toronto manager.

This leaves Warsaw and the situation tells us that Brenda Roche from head office will go over as the temporary manager.

Now you are ready to fill in the staffing chart.

7.2 Exercises

EXERCISE 7.1

Situation: You have recently joined the firm of Stelzer International and your manager is telling you about the foreign branches.

'Apart from our head office in London we have 3 offices abroad at present. These are in Toronto, Ho Chi Minh City and Oslo. The Toronto office opened in 1999. Oslo opened 2 years earlier and Ho Chi Minh City a year after Oslo. Oskar Gunnarsen is in charge of the Oslo office. The other 2 are managed by Hannah Samuels and Lee Cheng. Lee is a native of Ho Chi Minh, so he fits in very well there. We plan to open another office this year in Warsaw. We have not appointed a manager there yet; Brenda Roche from head office will go over there as manager and train someone to take over from her. Well, that's the present picture.'

Task: Use the information above to complete the Staffing Chart below in order of opening.

STELZER INTERNATIONAL
Staffing chart

Branch	Year of opening	Name of manager

Check your answers before you start the next exercise.
The correct answers and comment for this exercise are on page 190.

EXERCISE 7.2

Situation: You work for an electronics company in London. Your manager has left you a message on his voicemail.

'Will you please check my diary for free dates in the last 2 weeks of February? Hans Kleidermann of Stuttgart Systems wants me to visit their factory on the 16th or the 17th – it must be on a Wednesday! On the following Monday I have invited Barbara Gallo to our offices for a 2 pm meeting. On the 23rd (2 days later) I fly to Hanoi to see Lee Tan. I'll be there until Thursday night. Jack Bowen is meeting me the day after in Phnom Penh. Check it all for me, will you? Oh, I nearly forgot – Cesar Vaccaro wants to see me in Madrid on the 14th, or the Saturday after if I'm already engaged.'

Task: Complete the entries for the diary below.

Diary

February	Contact person	Place
Monday 14	Danielle Brisson	New York
Tuesday 15		
Wednesday 16		
Thursday 17		
Friday 18		
Saturday 19		
Sunday 20		
Monday 21		
Tuesday 22		
Wednesday 23		
Thursday 24		
Friday 25		
Saturday 26		
Sunday 27		
Monday 28		

Check your answers before you start the next exercise.
The correct answers and comment for this exercise are on page 191.

EXERCISE 7.3

Situation: You work as the Sales Manager for Singspiel Animal Feeds Ltd in Consett in the north of England. You have been asked to produce a clear chart of your company's departmental structure for a meeting of shareholders. Your Joint MD, Rotraut Singspiel, has left you the following notes and a partly completed chart (page 82).

Joint Managing Director's notes:

Well, starting at the very top, there is myself as Joint MD and I share responsibility with Robert Glover. My areas are Production and Personnel; Robert takes care of Sales and Plant Maintenance. We each have a Personal Assistant – Sandy Wane and Irene Lucic. Irene works with Robert.

There are 4 directors below us, one for each area. Walter Kort handles Production, Nazema Shah does Plant Maintenance. I have Peter Weiss and Robert has Cherry Langley as his other director.

The next tier is the managers, again one for each area of Production, Plant Maintenance, Personnel, and Sales, and they are, respectively, Allan Smith, Sam Levene, Otto Flick and...I hardly need to tell you the last of the 4, do I?

The assistants come at the bottom – 2 for each area. Your area has Raina Pelk as UK Sales Assistant, and Tom Pink deals with the foreign orders. Personnel has a Personnel Assistant and a Welfare Assistant – as you know, Colin Joseph does the first and his colleague is Angela Mottram. The other 2 areas' assistants just share the same job title. Kay Hamley and Bernard Brisson work in Production. Kurt Schmidt is on his own at the moment, because his opposite number, Peter Parker, left 2 days ago.

Task: Using the notes, fill in the blank spaces on the chart.

Write the names down in the 1 to 20 column below the chart.

SINGSPIEL ANIMAL FEEDS LTD
DEPARTMENT/STAFFING CHART

3	Joint MD	2	Personal Assistant
Sandy Wane	1	Robert Glover	4

Production Director	6	Sales Director	Plant Maintenance Director
5	7	Cherry Langley	8

Production Manager	10	Sales Manager	Plant Maintenance Manager
9	Otto Flick	11	12

Production Assistant	Personnel Assistant	14	15
Kay Hamley	13	Raina Pelk	Kurt Schmidt

Production Assistant	17	Sales Assistant (foreign)	Plant Maintenance Assistant
16	18	19	20

Write the names/titles here:

No	Name of person or staffing title
1	
2	
3	
4	
5	
6	
7	
8	
9	

▶

No	Name of person or staffing title
10	
11	
12	
13	
14	
15	
16	
17	
18	
19	
20	

Check your answers before you start the next exercise.
Correct answers and comments are on pages 191–2.

EXERCISE 7.4

Situation: It is the morning of 23 January. You come into the office of the Sales and Administration Department of the Artemis Clothing Company where you work, and find the night security guard, Jackie Chan, waiting for you. The following conversation takes place:

'Good morning, Jackie.'
'Good morning, sir. We had a break-in last night; some new clothing was taken. Three whole racks of coats.'
'That was the order for Willis and Franks, worth over £5,000. When did it all happen?'
'Around 22.30 last night, sir. I was in my office across the yard. I heard a door bang and looked out. There were 3 men getting into a van.'
'Did you see the registration number?'
'Only part of it, sir. It was dirty. I noted down 664DKT. It was a Ford van, I know that.'
'Good. Well done. Have you notified the police?'
'I rang them at 22.40 and they arrived 15 minutes later.'
'What can you remember about the 3 men?'
'One was very tall. One had a beard, and walked with a limp. I don't know any more.'
'Never mind, well done. And thanks for waiting to tell me.'

You check the missing items. The thieves have taken 150 ladies' coats and 100 men's jackets.

Your company address in Birmingham is: Unit 6, Canal Wharf, and the postcode is BM5 6JD.

Task: Use the information above to complete the Theft Report Form below.

ARTEMIS CLOTHING COMPANY
Theft Report Form
(COMPLETE IN CAPITALS)

1 Date of incident

2 Time of incident

3 Incident reported by (name and dept)

4 Were police informed?

5 Time police arrived

6 Description of intruders

7 Was a vehicle involved?

8 Description of vehicle

9 Name(s) of witnesses*

10 Description of stolen goods

11 Estimated value of goods

12 Report completed by

                        Name

                        Department

                        Signature

                        Date

* other than person named in 3 above

Check your answers before you start the next exercise.
Correct answers and comments are on pages 192–3.

EXERCISE 7.5

Situation: You work for Elite Cars Ltd, a company which provides a service for business men and women, collecting them by car from the airports in Paris, and delivering them to their hotel in the centre of the city. The manager gives you the following notes:

'There are just 4 people to collect from Charles de Gaulle airport today. Mr Walter Langlauf is arriving from Warsaw on flight number LO5293, landing time 10.00 hrs. He will meet a colleague, Helga Weiss. She is coming from Stockholm on flight SK525. Her arrival time is 10 minutes after his. He is attending a conference and is staying at the Majestic; she is meeting her daughter at the Ritz. I'm sure they can share a car. The other two are David Lowe, arriving at 11.40 hrs from London, and Melissa Crane coming on AMM1465 at 12.30 hrs from Boston. Mr Lowe is on flight BA1605. He is staying at the Plaza and she is booked in at the Meridian. Make the list out in arrival time order. Oh, I nearly forgot. Mr Lowe mentioned that he needs an hour after he lands to talk to a colleague at the airport, so allow for that in your timings.'

As your manager leaves there is an e-mail from Melissa to say that she is now on flight AMM1560 which will be arriving 2 hours after her original time.

Task: Using the information above complete the Client collection schedule.

ELITE CARS LTD
Client collection schedule

Name	Time	Flight no	Arriving from	Hotel

Check your answers before you start the next exercise.
Correct answers and comments are on page 193.

EXERCISE 7.6

Situation: You are bringing your desk diary up to date for the next month.

Task: Use the notes below from your pocket diary, plus the details of regular meetings to complete the diary for February on the next page.

If you have no entry for a day, write 'free' against the date. If you have more than one entry for a day, **put the second entry in the same day of the following week.** Leave all weekends blank.

Write your entries as briefly as possible.

Pocket diary notes:

8 Feb	Sales assistant interviews
11 Feb	Out of office today and tomorrow
22 Feb	Meet Sunila Arshad
14 Feb	Margaret (secretary) birthday – flowers
8 Feb	Budget meeting
5 Feb	Complete sales report

Regular activities:

Every 1st and 3rd Wednesday of the month – Group training
Every 2nd and 4th Wednesday of the month – Lunch at golf club
Every 1st and last Thursday of the month – Charity committee
Tuesdays – Management meeting

Desk diary for February

Day	Date	Diary entry/appointment
Monday	1	
Tuesday	2	
Wednesday	3	
Thursday	4	
Friday	5	
Saturday	6	
Sunday	7	
Monday	8	
Tuesday	9	
Wednesday	10	
Thursday	11	
Friday	12	
Saturday	13	
Sunday	14	
Monday	15	
Tuesday	16	
Wednesday	17	
Thursday	18	
Friday	19	
Saturday	20	
Sunday	21	
Monday	22	
Tuesday	23	
Wednesday	24	
Thursday	25	
Friday	26	
Saturday	27	
Sunday	28	

Check your answers before you start the next exercise.
Correct answers and comments are on pages 193–4.

EXERCISE 7.7

Situation: You work on the reception desk at the Pines Hotel and Conference Centre in Brighton. You have just received the letter printed below.

DANBY CLARK plc
World-wide Marketing Consultants
6 London Wall
London EC1 5JJ

e-mail: danbyclark@compuserve.com

Tel: 0171-600-1111
Fax: 0171-600-1435

13 March 2000

The Booking Manager
Pines Hotel and Conference Centre
Marine Parade
Brighton BR3 4JH

Dear Sir

This year Danby Clark plc will host the UK Marketing Awards. I wish to book your Prince of Wales Suite for the afternoon of 20 July. We shall require exclusive use of the suite from 12.00 noon onwards. The whole event will last about 5 hours, but please allow a further hour to be on the safe side.

The awards ceremony will be attended by some 200 business persons. 60 of them will travel by train from London. Please arrange a coach transfer for them at 11.45 am.

We plan to start at 12.30 pm with a reception and drinks (champagne plus some non-alcoholic drinks, please). We want to start lunch an hour later (tables of 10 persons, please), and that must take no longer than one and a half hours. The awards will follow lunch, and should be completed in 2 hours.

We shall require a large TV screen and a video recorder.

Please invoice me personally at our head office.

Yours faithfully

Gail Kowalski

Gail Kowalski

Managing Director

Task: Use the information in the letter to complete the booking form.

PINES HOTEL AND CONFERENCE CENTRE

Conference booking form
(COMPLETE IN CAPITALS)

Name of company

Address

Telephone

Title of function

Date of function

Times   From   To

Suite

Number of persons

Meals required   Time

Number of tables

Other requirements   1

                                     2

                                     3

                                     4

Invoice to

Check your answers.
Correct answers and comments are on pages 194–5.

KEYNOTES

- Read the information very carefully.
- Understand precisely what you have to do.
- Work logically, and deal with one thing at a time.
- Use coloured pens to highlight information.
- Make sure that names, positions, times, etc, are accurately copied.

8

Language competence: structures, concepts and vocabulary

8.1 Introduction

The language exercises are written to help you to improve your command of simple business English as you work your way through the book.

The exercises focus on the different parts of speech and on the general vocabulary that is used in simple business situations.

Much of the content of the exercises is similar to the writing that you do in the letters and memos, Chapters 3 and 4.

These exercises should make you feel more confident in writing simple business English to the standard required for success in the English for Business First Level examination.

Try to complete one exercise in each work session.

Use your workbook, not the pages in the book. You may find it useful to repeat the exercises at regular intervals. This will help you to achieve a better command of the language.

The exercises are arranged as follows:

8.2	Verbs: tenses and forms	Exercises 8.1–8.14
8.3	Adjectives, adverbs and pronouns	Exercises 8.15–8.18
8.4	Subordinate clauses	Exercise 8.19
8.5	General vocabulary exercises	Exercises 8.20–8.25

The answers are given in Appendix 1, pages 195–204.

8.2 Verbs

EXERCISE 8.1: SIMPLE PRESENT

Choose the correct form of the verbs in brackets to complete the following sentences.

Example: I talk
           she works
           they train

1   The customer (telephones/telephone/telephoning) our office.

2   The photocopier usually (work/working/works) very well.

3   The interview (taking/take/takes) place at 11 o'clock today.

4   How (are/am/is) he today?

5   They (have/has/having) an appointment with the MD. They (hopes/hope/hoping) to complete the contract.

6   We (sends/sending/send) out invoices on Mondays.

7   On most days she (assists/assist/assisting) her supervisor.

8   They (offering/offers/offer) a discount for cash when we (buys/buying/buy) in bulk.

9   He (arrives/arriving/arrive) soon. His flight (am/is/are) late.

10 (Have/has/had) you a pen, please? I (wish/wishing/wishes) to write a note.

EXERCISE 8.2: PRESENT CONTINUOUS

Choose the correct form of the verbs in brackets to complete the following sentences.

Example: I am sending
            is she arriving?
            they are coming

1   I (arrive) at 11 o'clock and I (bring) the contract with me.

2   She (ask) for permission to leave early; she (meet) her son.

3   You (have) difficulty with the fax machine. It (work) badly.

4   They (walk) to the hotel and they (have) lunch there.

5   He (write) a letter to the delivery agent. He (complain) about the delay.

6   We (wait) for the taxi. It (take) us to the airport.

7   The bus (wait) outside. The driver (read) the newspaper.

8   The documents (come) by special courier before noon.

9   Some of the staff (lose) their jobs tomorrow. They (protest) to the MD. He (try) to find them jobs in another company.

10 We (hold) a competition today. All the staff (enter). The MD (give) a prize for the best entry. The winner (go) on a holiday to Italy.

EXERCISE 8.3: SIMPLE PAST

Choose the correct form of the verb to complete the following sentences.

Example: I ordered
            they arrived
            you completed

1   He (clap) his hands when he (hear) the result.

2   The planes (land) at 2-minute intervals.

3   The office lift (stop) working at noon yesterday. It (start) again at teatime.

4   I (book) the tickets last week. I (make) the hotel reservation at the same time.

5   She (complain) about the noise. I (tell) her to ignore it.

6   Yesterday we (interview) for a secretary. We (decide) not to appoint anyone.

7   The firm (advertise) its latest products on TV. We (show) the advertisement 6 times.

8 The parcel (weigh) 20 kilos. The post office (refuse) to handle it for us.

9 Our new MD (visit) the factory yesterday. She (bring) her daughter with her.

10 You (think) the order was for 1,000 boxes. The customer's letter (state) that he only (want) 100 boxes. You (despatch) too many boxes.

EXERCISE 8.4: PRESENT PERFECT

Choose the correct form of the verbs in brackets to complete the following sentences.

Example: I have ordered
you have completed
they have ended

1 We (write) to the Chairman and he (send) his reply.

2 The accountant (show) that our profits (fall).

3 She (arrive) by taxi. I (pay) the driver.

4 When you (finish) your typing you can go. I (complete) the other jobs.

5 We (invite) a number of customers. So far, seven (accept) our invitation.

6 He (refuse) our offer. He (take) his business to another firm.

7 We (establish) our new delivery system. The transport manager (train) all the delivery drivers.

8 She (repair) the photocopier, and she (leave) a new instruction manual.

9 Our staff magazine (introduce) a new feature about hobbies. Six members of staff (contribute) to the first article.

10 Our department (purchase) new desks and chairs for all staff. The supplier (take) all the old furniture.

EXERCISE 8.5: FUTURE EXPRESSED IN THE PRESENT TENSE WITH A TIME MARKER

Choose the correct form of the verbs in brackets to complete the following sentences.

Example: I am writing the report today.
She is arriving tomorrow.

1 We (come) to your office (yesterday/last week/tomorrow).

2 The delivery van (arrive) at 10 o'clock in the (day/afternoon/morning).

3 The team (work) throughout the (hour/midnight/day).

4 I (ask) for permission to visit the factory (never/soon/earliest).

5 The complaints procedure (start) (last/every/next) month.

6 Six new employees (begin) work for us (today/yesterday/last year).

7 We (prepare) the conference room (then/formerly/immediately).

8 The wages department (prepare) your wage slip (the day before/tomorrow/next week).

9 All members of staff (go) to the celebration (next Tuesday/last Thursday/every week).

10 You (finish) your employment with us (an hour ago/in one hour/just then).

EXERCISE 8.6: 'SHALL' AND 'WILL'

Choose the correct form of the verbs in brackets to complete the following sentences.

Example: I *shall* send the fax.
            She *will* find the document.

Note: With the pronouns 'I' and 'We' both 'shall' and 'will' are now acceptable. Use 'will' with the pronouns 'you', 'he', 'she', and 'they'.

1 I (go) to their offices tomorrow.

2 The flight (take) 5 hours.

3 They (order) the meal shortly.

4 She (buy) a new computer.

5 You (receive) new instructions by e-mail.

6 We (try) to satisfy your request.

7 You and my secretary (meet) to arrange the conference.

8 The supplier (give) us a discount.

9 Many employees (take) their holidays in June.

10 The parts (arrive) by road.

EXERCISE 8.7: FUTURE EXPRESSED WITH 'GOING TO'

Rewrite the sentences in Exercise 8.6, using the the words 'going to'.

1 I am going to go to their offices tomorrow.

2

3

4

5

6

7

8

9

10

EXERCISE 8.8: IMPERATIVES

This exercise gives practice in *telling* someone to do something.

Example: *Please refer* to my letter.
            Meet me at the train station.

Write the following in the correct word order. To help you, the key *telling* word for the sentence is in italics.

1 office documents my to please the *bring* now

2 avoid it order to breaking in, care *carry* with parcel the

3 meeting the the at please visitors of *count* number

4 today the *visit* department please despatch

5 noon before the article please desk my on *place*

6 invitations hand by *write* the

7 machine *order* the please replacement soon as as possible

8 month this workforce have earned bonus a they *tell* the please

9 supervisor to please the *go* and mistake your *apologise* for

10 door close the please to *remember*; locked sure door is the *make*

EXERCISE 8.9

This exercise gives you practice in using the words:

can
may
must
would
will.

Complete the following sentences, using these words.

Example: If you took out a contract, we *would* certainly offer a discount.

1 If you took out a contract, we (   ) certainly offer a discount.

2 You (   ) finish your work before you leave the office.

3 If you are not sure, you (   ) always ask for advice.

4 It is not certain, but we (   ) ask for a reference.

5 If he did not come by air, then he (   ) probably come by train.

6 If he does not come by train, he (   ) probably catch a plane.

7 You (   ) call me on my mobile 24 hours a day.

8 You (   ) be right, but it is difficult to decide at the moment.

9 The deadline is 3 o'clock, so we (   ) reach a decision now.

10 I (   ) ensure personally that all the parts are delivered.

11 In ordinary circumstances that (   ) do very well.

12 (   ) I take the documents now, please?

13 (   ) you leave so early? It is only 2 o'clock.

14 If you had a problem with the copier, we (   ) send someone at once.

15 If you have a problem, we (   ) send someone at once.

16 She has no choice in the matter; she (   ) sign the contract today.

17 Why (   ) you go? It is a meeting for assistants.

18 If your service does not improve, we (   ) decide to go to another firm.

19 We are 100% reliable and therefore we (   ) guarantee total satisfaction.

20 They (   ) vote to strike, so I (   ) go there at once.

8.3 Adjectives, adverbs and pronouns

EXERCISE 8.10: POSSESSIVE ADJECTIVES

Using the adjectives:

my	your
his	her
our	your
their.	

Choose the correct adjective to place in the brackets to complete the following sentences.

1 If you want (   ) opinion, just ask me.

2 Has he completed all (   ) work for the day?

3 She will soon realise that (   ) new job is very demanding.

4 Have Tom and Anna left? (   ) cars are still in the car park.

5 If you give me (   ) address, I will write to them.

6 Is (   ) hair untidy? I want to make a good impression.

7 I cannot contact Mrs Petrangeli. (   ) mobile phone must be switched off.

8 Please accept (   ) congratulations. We think (   ) new book is very good.

9 Please tell Jane that (   ) appointment with him is for 2 o'clock.

10 Did Anna write this letter? Why must I correct (   ) mistakes?

11 I went to Johnson's Ltd yesterday and ate in (   ) executive dining room.

12 The owner, Carlo Trevino, says that (   ) ideas are up to date, but a lot of (   ) equipment is too old.

13 If you need to write to Janet and James, I will give you (   ) addresses before I leave.

14 We have spoken to (   ) own lawyers about the matter. That is what we pay them for.

15 Where is Ravi Arshad? He has not finished (   ) report.

16 Please help us and ask the theatre to change (   ) tickets; we are going to be late.

17 You cannot help her. (   ) decision to leave is her own.

18 I want them to know that (   ) car is at (   ) disposal.

19 She always carries (   ) handbag on (   ) left shoulder.

20 Unlike John I like to take (   ) time. (   ) method is to rush into things.

EXERCISE 8.11: DEMONSTRATIVE ADJECTIVES

Using the adjectives:

this	that
these	those

Choose the correct adjective from those above to write in the brackets and complete the following sentences.

1 (   ) book here is a very good guide.

2 I like (   ) computer games over there.

3   Which desk would you like? (   ) one here, or the one over there?

4   (   ) tools I have here are very useful.

5   Does (   ) road we are on take us to Rome?

6   I have told you before about Quickfast. (   ) firm is not reliable.

7   May I show you (   ) documents I mentioned yesterday?

8   Which of you has written (   ) report over there on my desk?

9   I do not like (   ) airport. It is always as busy as this.

10 She says she will send (   ) files you asked for at once.

11 I do not like (   ) suggestions you made yesterday. I prefer (   ) ideas that Hannah has just given to me.

12 (   ) dress I am wearing is most suitable.

13 (   ) shoes you showed me last night will match (   ) dress I wore on Friday.

14 Do not lose (   ) plan I gave you.

15 Some of (   ) staff we met yesterday are very clever.

16 (   ) parcels here are for immediate despatch, but (   ) crates in the corner can go tomorrow.

17 (   ) decisions we took yesterday are final. We cannot keep having (   ) uncertainties.

18 If you will take (   ) people over there, I will look after (   ) people here.

19 (   ) drawings in my hand are for the new factory.

20 (   ) word processor next door is very old. Replace it with one of (   ) word processors we bought yesterday.

EXERCISE 8.12: DESCRIPTIVE ADJECTIVES, COMPARATIVE

Complete the following sentences by choosing the correct word to go in the brackets.

For numbers 1 to 5, use only one of these words

good
better
best.

For numbers 6 to 10, use only one of these words

some
more
most.

For numbers 11 to 15 use only one of these words

little
less
least.

1   Last month's sales figures were very (good, better, best), but this month's are even (good, better, best).

2   He is the (   ) worker in this department, but Ann Park over Sales is even (   ).

3   The attitude of our staff is very (   ); in fact, it could not be (   ).

4   This is without doubt the (   ) photocopier on the market.

5   We make many (   ) products, but on a few occasions we make something that is (   ).

6   There is (   ) paper on the desk, and there is (   ) in the drawer.

7   There are (   ) people in the USA than in Norway.

8   I wish to buy (   ) books, please. Do you have any (   ) downstairs?

9   Of all the people I work with, I like Tina the (   ).

10 The (   ) I see her, the (   ) I like her style.

11 I have brought you a (   ) present.

12 There is (   ) paper in the stockroom than I thought there was.

13 It is the (   ) I can do to say thank you.

14 Most employees are paid (   ) than yourself.

15 Of all the jobs we have to do, this is the (   ) important.

EXERCISE 8.13: LOCATIVE ADVERBS (PLACE)

Complete the following sentences by choosing the correct word to go in the brackets. Choose from these words:

here   there
anywhere   everywhere
inside   outside.

1   It is very hot in the office today. Shall we go (   ) for a while?

2   I'm getting cold out here. Shall we go back (   ) the building?

3   (   ) you look, you can see people working.

4   I have looked (   ) for that file, but I cannot find it.

5   There are no restrictions; you can go (   ) you like in the building.

6   Did you come (   ) on the train?

7   I followed instructions and went (   ) by the shortest route.

8   When we stood (   ) in the entrance hall, we saw no-one, but as soon as we went (   ) there were people (   ) you looked.

9   He is a real globe-trotter. He travels (   ) in the world. He will go (   ) you want him to go.

10 I have looked (   ) for Tom, but I cannot find him (   ). Do you think he came (   ) first or went straight (   )?

EXERCISE 8.14: POSSESSIVE PRONOUNS

Using the words:

mine   your
his   hers
ours   yours
theirs.

Complete the following sentences by writing one of the words above in the brackets.

1   This calculator is (   ); (   ) is on the desk, Jane.

2   John bought the pen, so it must be (   ), even though Anna says it is (   ).

3   Both Ali and Petra did the work, so the responsibility is (   ).

4   You are late for lunch. We have already eaten (   ), but (   ) has gone cold.

5   We have done nothing wrong. The mistake must be (   ), Janet.

6   The decision we make is (   ); the decision the rest make is (   ).

7   Why can Lucia and Paolo never agree if something is (   ) or (   )?

8   I don't like my calculator, Hannah. Can I please borrow (   )?

9   The assistant managers are angry. The managers have BMWs, but (   ) are only Volvos.

10 Since this letter is addressed to me, it must be (   ).

11 I have just seen my new office, Helga. Have you seen (   ) yet?

12 Rozi says she is sure the bag is (   ). She saw you buy it last week.

13 Salma and Anisha have a really nice office. I envy them. I really prefer (   ) to (   ).

14 We have booked tickets on the 3 o'clock train. Do you think that train on platform 2 will be (   )?

15 I am happy with my working hours, Andy, but you are lucky, because (   ) are more convenient than mine.

16 Bob and Rupert will have to leave their office; it is (   ) that I want.

17 Barbara lost a bag like that last week. I am sure it is (   ).

18 The MD has just given me my new car. He says he will give you (   ) tomorrow.

19 If you want the job, then it is (   ).

20 The sales team have worked hard to win the contract. The success is (   ) alone.

EXERCISE 8.15: INDEFINITE PRONOUNS

Using the words:

everyone	anyone	something
everybody	no-one	anything
nobody	someone	
everything	nothing.	

Complete the following sentences by writing the correct word in the brackets.

1   There is (   ) I want you to do for me.

2   (   ) sincerely hopes that the meeting is a success.

3   Is there (   ) who can tell me what to do?

4   It is ridiculous. I have asked (   ) in the office and (   ) knows how to send an e-mail.

5   I have all the information. There is (   ) more that I need.

6   There is (   ) wrong with the delivery system. (   ) on our list is complaining.

7   Is (   ) doing (   ) about this broken fax machine?

8   This fax machine has been broken for 3 weeks. Will (   ) please do (   ) about it?

9   (   ) must enter my room without knocking.

10 (   ) has taken the safe key and not returned it. Does (   ) know (   ) about it?

11 I want to see (   ) in my office now. (   ) must ignore this request. I have (   ) important to tell you all.

12 If you have worked for 5 years, you receive a bonus. This applies to (   ).

13 Could (   ) please close that door?

14 I hope that (   ) is to your satisfaction.

15 It seems to be well planned. I cannot think of (   ) else that needs doing or (   ) else to write to.

16 This is our secret. You must tell (   ) else.

17 I cannot keep the secret. I must tell (   ) else.

18 I have told you (   ) I know about it.

19 The MD shook hands with (   ) and congratulated them.

20 (   ) must work hard this week. There is (   ) coming to inspect the firm. The MD wants (   ) to go wrong. (   ) depends on making a good impression.

8.4 Subordinate clauses

EXERCISE 8.16: SUBORDINATE CLAUSES

Using the words

if	that
because	where
when	until.

Complete the following sentences, using one of the words listed above.

1 I think I have covered everything, but please ring me (   ) you have further questions.

2 He told me (   ) he would find a solution to the problem.

3 We cannot attend the meeting, (   ) our MD is on holiday.

4 Do you know (   ) you are going after you leave Seattle?

5 (   ) I receive your order, I shall despatch it at once.

6 It is very important (   ) we all agree on the matter.

7 (   ) plans are not yet complete, I cannot tell you any more.

8 Did he say (   ) he was taking the drawings to?

9 The hotel will be booked, (   ) there is enough money.

10 (   ) you do not do as we ask, we cannot make the payment.

11 She was sacked, (   ) she refused to work overtime.

12 You must wait in the hall, (   ) you are sent for.

13 You must go to the canteen, (   ) the visitors are waiting for you.

14 (   ) you wish to place an order, please telephone us today.

15 He could not leave the hotel, (   ) the fax came through.

16 He has not told us, (   ) he will be arriving.

17 She will do the extra work, (   ) I ask her nicely.

18 It is for these reasons (   ) we must increase production.

19 John will not come to work today, (   ) he has a cold.

20 Shall we go somewhere quiet, (   ) we can discuss the matter?

8.5 General vocabulary

EXERCISE 8.17: LOCATION, DISTANCE, DIRECTIONS

Supply suitable words to complete the following sentences. For instance, a suitable word to complete number 1 would be 'north'.

1 Scotland is situated to the (   ) of England.

2 Mexico is situated to the (   ) of the USA.

3 The sun always sets in the (   ).

4 Europeans describe Japan as part of the Far (   ).

5 The office is very (   ) to the airport.

6 How (   ) is it to your office? A few miles?

7 Take the first turning on the (   ), then go (   ) ahead for 100 metres.

8 Remember to turn (   ), not left at the bank.

9 Tuesday is the day after (   ).

10 At the (   ) we usually go to the beach.

11 The day after (   ) is Wednesday.

12 Can you please tell me the (   )? Is it 3 o'clock yet?

13 He will be arriving at 6 o'(   ).

14 How many (   ) are there in an hour? There are 60.

15 In a race every (   ) counts.

16 I will not repeat myself. I shall say this only (   ).

17 The machine broke down on Monday and on Friday. It has broken down (   ).

18 The race (   ) at 2 o'clock. It (   ) at 4 o'clock.

19 What was the winner's (   ) time? It was under 2 hours.

20 You must (   ) to keep this a secret.

EXERCISE 8.18

Complete the following sentences by using one of the following words:

long   wide
weigh   weight
tall(er)   small(er),
short(er)   heavy.

1 How (   ) is this road? 2 kilometers.

2 Is this shelf (   ) enough for those files?

3 How much does the fax machine (   )? About 22 kilos.

4 Don't worry. It's only a (   ) problem.

5 The Eiffel Tower in Paris is a very (   ) building.

6 In a very (   ) time he will be promoted.

7 How (   ) is this bicycle? Does it (   ) more than 10 kilos?

8 Can you stretch your arms out (   )?

9 Your desk is 2 meters long; mine is 1.5 meters long. Mine is (   ) than yours.

10 I do not wish to keep you, so my speech will be quite (   ).

Complete these using one of the following words:

easy   difficult
expensive   cheap
better   worse.

11 These envelopes are quite (   ). They cost 50 cents each.

12 Our policy is to buy (   ) machines and replace them often.

13 The job is not an (   ) one. It calls for hard work.

14 Because of his strong views, he is a (   ) person to work with.

15 Thanking people is good, but praising them is (   ).

16 The July sales figures are bad, but the figures for June are even (   ).

17 All you have to do is sign it. It is not a (   ) task.

18 These envelopes are (   ). I expected them to be much more.

19 He should like his watch. It was quite (   ).

20 Now that we have the loan, I am sure things will get (   ).

EXERCISE 8.19

Supply suitable words for the gaps in the following passage of conversation.

Afternoon in the office

Dieter:
Good (   ), Janet. Can I (   ) you to Mrs Palmieri, our new Sales (   )?
I have (   ) her to look round the Production (   ).

Janet:
Good (   ), Mrs Palmieri. I am very (   ) to meet you. We have (   ) a lot about you. I look
(   ) very much to (   ) with you.

Mrs Palmieri:
It's a great (   ) to meet you, Janet. Please (   ) me Anna. I am sure I shall (   ) working
with you all. Will you be (   ) the meeting later this (   )?

Janet:
No, I'm afraid I must give my (   ). I have to (   ) in an hour. I am catching a (   ) to New
York. I hope my secretary has (   ) my seat. Dieter, before I (   ), will you take care of
Saturday's (   ) at the Plaza (   ) in Brighton? Make sure you (   ) yourself to Farida
Shah. She is the hotel (   ) and she promised to give us the very (   ) conference room. Well,
I (   ) be on my (   ). I have some (   ) to write before I (   ).

Dieter:
Don't worry, Janet. I'll (   ) care of everything at the (   ). Now, Anna, I'll give you a quick
(   ) of the (   ) department.

Mrs Palmieri:
(   ) you very (   ), Dieter. And thank you, (   ). Have a good (   ) in New York. I (   ) I
was (   ) myself. It's a very exciting (   ). I have a daughter who (   ) in Washington.
Perhaps we can have a (   ) about it when you (   ). Right, Dieter, lead on. You are my (   )
for the next half (   ).

EXERCISE 8.20

Supply suitable words to fill the gaps in the following passage of conversation.

At the conference

Davina Kaur is talking to Paul Levkas.

Davina:
Hello, Paul. I was (   ) you would be at the (   ). Do you (   ) me? We met a few days
(   ) at the music (   ).

Paul:
Of course, I (   ) you (   ) well indeed. You made the (   ) to the conductor on (   ) of
your firm. Your short (   ) was very entertaining. How (   ) you today?

Davina:
I'm very (   ), thank you. You look very well (   ). I'm so (   ) that we have (   ) again.
I (   ) to ask your (   ) about a very (   ) matter.

Paul:
If I (   ) be of some (   ), please tell me (   ) it.

Davina:
Well, you (   ) I work for Sissioni Perfumes. In fact, I've just been (   ) the position of
Marketing (   ). But the truth is, I don't (   ) to work for them any (   ). I'm not happy with the
(   ) they use. They are old fashioned and I would also (   ) a job with less travelling. I have
two sons and a (   ) and I want to spend more (   ) with (   ). So what I really (   ) is to
set up my own (   ). Can you give me some (   ) on how to (   ) that?

Paul:
Yes, I (   ). I had my (   ) business for a (   ) of years before I took the (   ) here. It
(   ) be better if we arranged an (   ) at my office. Or I (   ) meet you for lunch or (   )
one evening. I can give you the (   ) of some useful (   ). What about (   ) Wednesday?

Davina:
I'm (   ), Paul, I was watching that man over (   ). Can you (   ) what you just said, please?

Paul:
I was (   ) we (   ) meet next Wednesday.

Davina:
That's a (   ) idea. (   ) is my mobile number. Please (   ) me a call soon. I shall (   )
forward to (   ) from you. Goodbye for (   ).

EXERCISE 8.21

Rearrange the mixed up words below to make complete and meaningful sentences. The first word
of each sentence appears in **bold** letters to help you. Some of the last words in the more difficult
sentences are also shown in *italics*.

1 please you that again **can** say?
2 reply looking **I** your am early to forward
3 hotel *taxi* not would to travel the **I** by rather
4 want does **what** me problem do to the about he?
5 lunch was **that** had pleasant yesterday we very a

6 when deliver **can** tell *goods* us the will you they?

7 *department* colleagues number a am **I** production the to inviting of

8 her she that very appointment missed was sorry **she**

9 help soon hope **we** of be can further very we

10 you pleasure been skills **it** teaching has a these all

Part 3
Resources

9

Situations/tasks, checklists, build-up sheets and final versions

9.1 Letters

Letter-writing situation/task 1

Situation: You work as Assistant Sales Manager for Cybergames Ltd, which designs original training games for business organisations. You are planning an exclusive half-day demonstration of your new games, 'Takeover' and 'Marketing Manager'. This will take place at the head office for special customers only. Your Chief Designer, Ms Pauline Davi, will open the demonstration. There will also be a buffet lunch.

Your company is based at:

44 Regent Street, London WC1 2EE.

Task: Write a letter of invitation to Mr Roland Jenks, the Sales Director for Business Lines Ltd who, you hope, will market the new games. Include details such as date, times, venue, etc, plus a timetable for the half day. Give him a brief description of the new games.

The address of Business Lines Ltd is:

2 Bridge Street, Oxford, OX2 4JF.

You may invent any details that you feel are necessary.

Letter-writing situation/task 2

Situation: Your manager at Continental Furnishings, 4 Rupert Street, Bolton, BL4 6JH, has asked you to reserve display space at the Summer Furniture Exhibition in Augsburg, Germany. This takes place over a 3-day period at the Conference and Exhibition Centre in the city. You need to book:

- 5 display areas
- an office area to accommodate 3 staff
- the services of a lighting technician
- overnight accommodation for 2 staff for 2 nights.

Task: Write a letter to the Exhibition Secretary, Mr Gerhard Strauss, detailing all your needs. Ask for early confirmation of the booking and for the invoice to be sent to your Accounts Department. The address of the centre is:

Bahnhofstrasse 77, 86399 Augsburg, Germany.

You may invent any details that you feel are necessary.

Letter-writing situation/task 3

Situation: You work in the Sales Department of Starlight Perfumes Ltd which manufactures ladies' perfumes. You are looking to establish a market in Eastern Europe. Recently in London you met Mrs Liliana Vucic, who is Chief Buyer for a chain of department stores in Jugoslavia. Her contact address is:

64 Skadalije, 11000 Belgrade.

Task: Write a letter to Liliana Vucic from your offices at 4 Rosewood Square, Chelsea, London SW4 6BJ.

Tell her about your products and ask for her advice on establishing a new market in Eastern Europe.

You may invent any details that you feel are necessary.

Letter-writing situation/task 4

Situation: Your company, Antico Accountants, which is situated at:

Arenales 1880, in the city of Martinez in Argentina

has received an estimate for new furniture for 4 of your branch offices. The estimate is wrong for the following reasons:

- 1 office has not been included in the estimate
- only half the desks you need have been quoted
- the delivery date is 2 weeks later than requested.

You have tried to telephone the firm supplying the estimate without success.

Task: Write a letter to the Sales Manager of Alonso Office Supplies. Point out the mistakes and state exactly what you require. Mention the correct delivery date. The address of the firm is:

Avellanada 460, San Isidro, Buenos Aires, Argentina.

You may invent any details that you feel are necessary.

Letter-writing situation/task 5

Situation: You are employed by the Scottish Clothing Company based in Edinburgh, Scotland. An important new German customer, Timpops and Sons, has written to complain about a missing order for 250 Scottish caps. The firm is demanding compensation for loss of sales. Timpops is a customer you want to keep in future.

Task: From your head office at 84 Castle Street, Edinburgh EB2 6AJ, write a letter to the Manager of Timpops. Say what has happened to the order and tell her when delivery will take place. The address to write to is:

Bismarckstrasse 45–53, 42115 Wuppertal.

You may invent any details that you feel are necessary.

Letter-writing situation/task 6

Situation: This year your firm, Sparks Electronics, celebrates 25 years in business. You are holding a celebration party at a local hotel – reception, dinner, and dancing for staff and customers. Your Chairman wants a famous television personality to be chief guest and speaker. His first choice was not able to attend, and he now wants Mrs Helena Papas, who has a daily chat show on Sky TV.

Task: From your address at 388 Baker Street, London WC2 2EH, write a letter of invitation to Mrs Papas giving details of the event and a brief timetable for the evening. An early reply is essential. Mrs Papas' business address is:

Sky TV, Satellite House, Kew Road, London SW9 4AB.

You may invent any details that you feel are necessary.

Letter-writing situation/task 7

Situation: You work for International Plastics Ltd in Dundee, Scotland. Last week you flew to Stockholm in Sweden with a local airline, Tartanair. You were unhappy with the flight – delayed departure, no upgrade to Business class, poor service, and a very rude flight attendant when you complained.

Task: From your head office address, which is 84 Church Street, Dundee DD2 4YS, write a letter to the Customer Services Manager at Tartanair. Detail your experiences and ask her for some compensation. Point out that any future bookings from your firm will depend on their response. The address to write to is:

Tartanair House, 2 The Lapwings, Glasgow GL1 4BJ.

You may invent any details that you feel are necessary.

Letter-writing situation/task 8

Situation: You work for Meridian Carpets Ltd, whose address is:

4 Station Yard, Tewkesbury, TK3 4DN.

You have received a request from a women's group, Women Working from Home, for a tour of your factory. Your MD, Mrs Indira Patel, has agreed to a 3-hour visit (maximum 15 persons). The visit, which will start from the reception area, will include:

- welcome with coffee
- a talk by the chief designer, Sandy Tate
- a full tour of the factory
- lunch with the Sales Chief.

The visit is arranged for Tuesday 26 March, starting at 9.30 am.

Task: Write a letter replying to the Chairperson of the group, Mrs Anita Kapaldi, giving her full details of the agreed visit. Her address is:

The Old Post Office, Brockhampton, Cheltenham CH4 2BR.

You may invent any details that you feel are necessary.

Letter-writing situation/task 9

Situation: As an assistant in the Accounts Section at the Tianhenman Plaza Hotel in Beijing you have to deal from time to time with complaints about bills. An American company, Timewise Ltd, has sent back an invoice sent by the hotel for a 3-night stay by Mrs Hilary DuPont, their Chief Buyer. They complain that the charges for the room, food ordered, and telephone calls are too high.

Task: From your address in Beijing, which is:

44 Wangfujing Avenue, Beijing 10006

Write a letter of reply to the Senior Accountant at the firm and explain the high charges. Give details of the requests by Mrs DuPont which account for the unexpected charges. The address of Timewise Ltd, a customer whose valuable account you do not want to lose, is:

68 Union Square, New York 46150, USA.

You may invent any details that you feel are necessary.

Letter-writing situation/task 10

Situation: You work as an administrative assistant at the Gunter Hopp Fitness and Leisure Club, situated at:

Königinstrasse 54, 11203 Berlin.

Your manager is Herr Rudi Barenbohm and he has given you a list of candidates for a vacancy at the club. Interviews will take place on 16 November. Before the interviews, which start at 14.00 hrs, there will be a tour of the club and a meeting with other staff. These activities will take an hour, followed by the interviews which will be in alphabetical order.

Task: Write a letter of invitation to one of the candidates, Ms Natasha Braun, giving details and timings for the afternoon. Her address is:

Michelangelostrasse 19, 10409 Berlin.

Rudi has asked you to remind all candidates to bring along their qualification certificates.

You may invent any details that you feel are necessary.

Letter-writing situation/task 1: checklist

1 LAYOUT		
Name of writer	Student's name	
Address of writer	Cybergames Ltd 44 Regent Street London WC1 2EE	
Name of addressee	Mr Roland Jenks	
Inside address	Sales Director Business Lines Ltd 2 Bridge Street Oxford OX2 4JF	
Salutation	Dear Mr Jenks	
Complimentary close	Yours sincerely	
Suitable date	Date of examination	
2 CONTENT		
Main subject of letter	Demonstration of new business games	
Key points	1 Invitation to demonstration	4 Attendance of Chief Designer
	2 'Takeover' and 'Marketing Manager'	5 Timetable for morning
	3 Date/times/venue	6 Hope addressee can attend
Additional details	Special customers only invited	
Additional invented details	1 'Takeover' – all the problems of taking over a company	3 Arrival, coffee, introduction of games
	2 'Marketing Manager' – methods for success in positive team building	4 'Hands-on' testing, questions, lunch
Opening sentence	I write to invite you to the presentation of our latest business games	
Closing sentence	I look forward to the pleasure of seeing you at the demonstration	
3 STYLE AND TONE		
Writer/addressee relationship	Assistant Manager writing to Sales Director and valued customer	
Purpose of letter	To ensure the attendance of Mr Jenks at the demonstration	
Suitable phrases	1 exclusive occasion	4 learn a lot from both games
	2 most valued customers	5 and at same time enjoyable
	3 sure you will enjoy	6 look forward to the pleasure

Letter-writing situation/task 2: checklist

1 LAYOUT		
Name of writer	Student's name	
Address of writer	Continental Furnishings 4 Rupert Street Bolton BL4 6JH	
Name of addressee	Mr Gerhard Strauss	
Inside address	Conference and Exhibition Centre Bahnhofstrasse 77 86399 Augsburg Germany	
Salutation	Dear Mr Strauss	
Complimentary close	Yours sincerely	
Suitable date	Date of examination	

2 CONTENT		
Main subject of letter	Request for exhibition space and accommodation	
Key points	1 5 display areas	4 2 nights accommodation for 2 persons
	2 office area for 3 staff	5 early confirmation
	3 lighting technician	6 invoice Accounts Department
Additional details	3 living areas, 2 bedrooms	
Additional invented details	1 attended last year	3 looking for further new customers
	2 several orders taken last year	4
Opening sentence	I wish to reserve display space and accommodation for the summer exhibition	
Closing sentence	I look forward to your early confirmation of our booking	

3 STYLE AND TONE		
Writer/addressee relationship	Assistant Manager to conference organiser/business-like, respectful	
Purpose of letter	To secure reserved space and accommodation	
Suitable phrases	1 we shall require	4 please send invoice
	2 found last year enjoyable	5 more orders from German firms
	3 and successful for business	6

Letter-writing situation/task 3: checklist

1 LAYOUT			
Name of writer	Student's name		
Address of writer	Starlight Perfumes 4 Rosewood Square Chelsea London SW4 6BJ		
Name of addressee	Mrs Liliana Vucic		
Inside address	64 Skadalije 11000 Belgrade Yugoslavia		
Salutation	Dear Mrs Vucic		
Complimentary close	Yours sincerely		
Suitable date	Date of examination		
2 CONTENT			
Main subject of letter	Advice on new markets for perfumes		
Key points	1 Recent meeting in London		4 Outline Starlight product range
	2 Chief Buyer for department stores		5 Ask for advice
	3 Starlight seeking new markets		6
Additional details	Mrs Vucic expert in her field		Enjoyed meeting and talking to her
Additional invented details	1 Starlight covers all age ranges		3 Firm looking for European agent
	2 New perfume called 'Eastern Sunset'		4
Opening sentence	It was a great pleasure to meet you recently in London		
Closing sentence	I look forward to receiving your suggestions and advice		
3 STYLE AND TONE			
Writer/addressee relationship	Asst Sales Manager to Chief Buyer/respectful, warm, complimentary		
Purpose of letter	To gain advice and hopefully strengthen connection		
Suitable phrases	1 you 'opened my eyes' to opportunity		4 your valuable advice
	2 left feeling very enthusiastic		5 your considerable experience in field
	3 wide range of perfumes		6 would be most welcome

Letter-writing situation/task 4: checklist

1 LAYOUT		
Name of writer	Student's name	
Address of writer	Antico Accountants Arenales 1880 Martinez City Argentina	
Name of addressee	The Sales Manager	
Inside address	Alonso Office Supplies Avellanada 460 San Isidro Buenos Aires Argentina	
Salutation	Dear Sir	
Complimentary close	Yours faithfully	
Suitable date	Date of examination	

2 CONTENT		
Main subject of letter	Wrong estimate for office furniture	
Key points	1 estimate for furniture wrong	4 only half the desks ordered
	2 for 4 branch offices	5 wrong delivery date
	3 only 3 offices in estimate	6 no telephone response
Additional details	Clear order instructions	Exact delivery date
Additional invented details	1 number of desks/chairs for each office	3 disappointed by poor service
	2 order worth thousands of dollars	4 expect better, or cancel order
Opening sentence	I regret to inform you that the estimate you sent is not correct	
Closing sentence	Please confirm by return that everything is now in order	

3 STYLE AND TONE		
Writer/addressee relationship	Asst Accounts/Sales to Sales Manager/formal, business-like, sharply to the point	
Purpose of letter	To correct inaccuracies and obtain improved service	
Suitable phrases	1 number of serious errors	4 our precise wishes
	2 clearly instructed	5 give serious attention to
	3 very disappointed	6 may consider cancelling

Letter-writing situation/task 5: checklist

1 LAYOUT		
Name of writer	Student's name	
Address of writer	Scottish Clothing Company 84 Castle Street Edinburgh EB2 6AJ	
Name of addressee	The Manager	
Inside address	Timpops and Sons Bismarckstrasse 45–53 42115 Wuppertal Germany	
Salutation	Dear Madam	
Complimentary close	Yours faithfully	
Suitable date	Date of examination	
2 CONTENT		
Main subject of letter	Apology for non-delivery of order	
Key points	1 order for 250 Scottish caps	4 accept sincere apologies
	2 checked our files	5 new delivery date confirmed as
	3 highly valued customer	6 additional 10% discount
Additional details		
Additional invented details	1 order held up in Despatch Dept	3 delivery inside 3 days
	2 computer showed your account in arrears	4 business relationship 15 years
Opening sentence	I was very sorry to learn that your order has not arrived	
Closing sentence	Please accept our sincere apologies again	
3 STYLE AND TONE		
Writer/addressee relationship	Asst Sales Manager to Manager/apologetic and reassuring	
Purpose of letter	To apologise, and assure customer of good service	
Suitable phrases	1 very sorry to learn	4 I have personally supervised
	2 inconvenience caused	5 delivery by special carrier
	3 error on computer records	6 continue to do good business

Letter-writing situation/task 6: checklist

1 LAYOUT		
Name of writer	Student's name	
Address of writer	Sparks Electronics 388 Baker Street London WC2 2EH	
Name of addressee	Mrs Helena Papas	
Inside address	Sky TV Satellite House Kew Road London SW9 4AB	
Salutation	Dear Mrs Papas	
Complimentary close	Yours sincerely	
Suitable date	Date of examination	

2 CONTENT		
Main subject of letter	Invitation to appear as chief guest and speaker	
Key points	1 25 years in business	4 timetable for evening
	2 celebration for staff and customers	5 daily TV chat show
	3 date and venue	6 Chairman's choice of speaker
Additional details	Early reply will be welcome	Do not mention 2nd choice!
Additional invented details	1 chat show much admired	3 choose own speech topic
	2 chosen for popularity/talent	4 speech around 30 minutes
Opening sentence	Sparks Electronics invite you to be chief guest....	
Closing sentence	I hope you will be able to accept our invitation	

3 STYLE AND TONE		
Writer/addressee relationship	Asst Manager to TV personality/admiring, warm, respectful	
Purpose of letter	To persuade the addressee to attend celebration	
Suitable phrases	1 enjoy your show	4 guests will be thrilled
	2 sure you will entertain	5 technology experts
	3 and stimulate	6 greatly look forward to

Letter-writing situation/task 7: checklist

1 LAYOUT		
Name of writer	Student's name	
Address of writer	International Plastics Ltd 84 Church Street Dundee DD2 4YS	
Name of addressee	The Customer Services Manager	
Inside address	Tartanair Tartanair House 2 The Lapwings Glasgow GL1 4BJ	
Salutation	Dear Madam	
Complimentary close	Yours faithfully	
Suitable date	Date of examination	

2 CONTENT		
Main subject of letter	Complaint about airline's poor service	
Key points	1 flight to Stockholm	4 complaint ignored
	2 flight no/date/time	5 request for compensation
	3 delays/poor service/ rudeness	6 further custom doubtful
Additional details		
Additional invented details	1 delay of 2 hours	3 attendant referred me to
	2 cold in-flight food	4 customer services
Opening sentence	I wish to register a strong complaint about my recent flight	
Closing sentence	I hope you will give serious consideration to my request	

3 STYLE AND TONE		
Writer/addressee relationship	Customer to Customer Services Manager	
Purpose of letter	To express dissatisfaction and request compensation	
Suitable phrases	1 very disappointed	4 other passengers angry
	2 nearly missed important meeting	5 attendant very rude
	3 food and service a disgrace	6 further booking unlikely

Letter-writing situation/task 8: checklist

1 LAYOUT		
Name of writer	Student's name	
Address of writer	Meridian Carpets Ltd 4 Station Yard Tewkesbury TK3 4DN	
Name of addressee	Mrs Anita Kapaldi	
Inside address	Women Working from Home The Old Post Office Brockhampton Cheltenham CH4 2BR	
Salutation	Dear Mrs Kapaldi	
Complimentary close	Yours sincerely	
Suitable date	Date of examination	

2 CONTENT		
Main subject of letter	Confirmation of factory visit for women's group	
Key points	1 Confirm acceptance by MD	4 Factory tour
	2 Date/time/start reception coffee	5 Lunch with Sales Chief
	3 Talk by Sandy Tate	6 Maximum 15 persons
Additional details	MD Mrs Indira Patel	
Additional invented details	1 staff used to having visitors	3 and show their skills
	2 always happy to talk	
Opening sentence	You will be pleased to hear that our MD has given permission for your group to visit our factory	
Closing sentence	We all look forward to seeing you on the 26 March	

3 STYLE AND TONE		
Writer/addressee relationship	Asst Manager to Chair of women's group/warm and friendly	
Purpose of letter	To confirm acceptance of request for visit and outline arrangements	
Suitable phrases	1 pleased to hear	4 welcome your comments
	2 15 max for safety reasons	5 you may wish to order
	3 find tour very interesting	

Letter-writing situation/task 9: checklist

1 LAYOUT		
Name of writer	Student's name	
Address of writer	Tianhenman Plaza Hotel 44 Wangfujing Avenue Beijing 10006	
Name of addressee	The Senior Accountant	
Inside address	Timewise Ltd 68 Union Square New York 46150 USA	
Salutation	Dear Sir	
Complimentary close	Yours faithfully	
Suitable date	Date of examination	

2 CONTENT		
Main subject of letter	Answering complaint about hotel charges	
Key points	1 letter re invoice for Mrs DuPont	4 Mrs DuPont's requests
	2 high charges for room and service	5 all items on invoice
	3 during 3-night stay	6 value your account highly
Additional details		
Additional invented details	1 Mrs DuPont entertained in room	3 banquet for 16 final evening
	2 drinks and snacks services	4 many telephone calls made
Opening sentence	Thank you for your letter concerning Mrs DuPont's invoice	
Closing sentence	We hope this explanation is helpful and look forward to continuing a good business relationship with your company	

3 STYLE AND TONE		
Writer/addressee relationship	Accounts Assistant to Senior Accountant/respectful, informative, firm	
Purpose of letter	To explain high charges and retain customer goodwill	
Suitable phrases	1 we apologise for distress	4 value for money services
	2 invoice clearly shows	5 we trust and hope
	3 Mrs DuPont wants the best	6 we look forward to

Letter-writing situation/task 10: checklist

1 LAYOUT			
Name of writer	Student's name		
Address of writer	Gunter Hopp Fitness and Leisure Club Königinstrasse 54 11203 Berlin		
Name of addressee	Ms Natasha Braun		
Inside address	Michelangelostrasse 19 10409 Berlin		
Salutation	Dear Ms Braun		
Complimentary close	Yours sincerely		
Suitable date	Date of examination		
2 CONTENT			
Main subject of letter	Inform about interview arrangements		
Key points	1 invite for interview as asst instructor	4 Mr R Barenbohm (Manager)	
	2 14.00 hrs on 16 November	5 alphabetical order interviews	
	3 1-hour tour, meet other staff	6 qualification certificates	
Additional details	Gunter Hopp Fitness Centre		
Additional invented details	1 4 other candidates	3 report to reception on arrival	
	2 enclose map and directions	4	
Opening sentence	I am pleased to invite you for interview on 16 November		
Closing sentence	I look forward to meeting you on 16 November		
3 STYLE AND TONE			
Writer/addressee relationship	Admin Assistant to job applicant/friendly and informative		
Purpose of letter	Detail interview arrangements; put candidate at ease		
Suitable phrases	1 shortlist of 5 candidates for position	4 please do not forget . . .	
	2 very successful club	5 prompt start at 13.00 hrs	
	3 friendly and helpful staff	6 any questions, please contact	

LETTER WRITING	CHECKLIST FOR SITUATION/TASK	
1 LAYOUT		
Name of writer		
Address of writer		
Name of addressee		
Inside address		
Salutation		
Complimentary close		
Suitable date		
2 CONTENT		
Main subject of letter		
Key points	1	4
	2	5
	3	6
Additional details		
Additional invented details	1	3
	2	4
Opening sentence		
Closing sentence		
3 STYLE AND TONE		
Writer/addressee relationship		
Purpose of letter		
Suitable phrases	1	4
	2	5
	3	6

Sample letter-writing build-up sheet for situation/task 1

Key points

We are holding a demonstration of our new business games. The games are 'Takeover' and 'Marketing Manager'. This will take place on 26 March starting at 10.00 am. Our Chief Designer will be present. I enclose a timetable. We hope you can attend.

(43 words)

Additional details

We are holding a demonstration of our new business games. The games are 'Takeover' and 'Marketing Manager'. This will take place on 26 March starting at 10.00 am. Our Chief Designer will be present. Special customers only are invited. I enclose a timetable. We hope you can attend.

(47 words)

Additional invented details

We are holding a demonstration of our new business games. The games are 'Takeover' and 'Marketing Manager'. This will take place at our head office on 26 March starting at 10.00 am. Our Chief Designer will be present. Special customers only are invited.

The timetable includes reception and coffee, introduction of games, hands-on testing, questions and lunch.

'Takeover' presents all the problems of taking over a company.

'Marketing Manager' contains the methods for success in positive team building.

We hope you can attend.

(83 words)

Sample letter-writing build-up sheet for situation/task 2

Key points

We request space and accommodation for the Summer Furniture Exhibition. We need 5 display areas and an office area for 3 staff. We need a lighting technician. We also need accommodation for 2 nights for 2 persons. Invoice our Accounts Department. Send early confirmation.

(39 words)

Additional details

We request space and accommodation for the Summer Furniture Exhibition. We need 5 display areas – 3 areas for living rooms and 2 areas for bedrooms – and an office area for 3 staff. We need a lighting technician. We also need accommodation for 2 nights for 2 persons. Invoice our Accounts Department. Send early confirmation.

(48 words)

Additional invented details

We request space and accommodation for the Summer Furniture Exhibition. We need 5 display areas – 3 areas for living rooms and 2 areas for bedrooms – and an office area for 3 staff. We need a lighting technician. We also need accommodation for 2 nights for 2 persons.

We attended last year and several orders were taken. We are looking for further new customers.

Invoice our Accounts Department. Send early confirmation.

(65 words)

Letter-writing build-up sheet student's blank for situation/task

Key points

Additional details

Additional invented details

Letter-writing situation/task 1: completed letter

Cybergames Ltd
44 Regent Street
London
WC1 2EE

Date of examination

Mr Roland Jenks
Sales Director
Business Lines Ltd
2 Bridge Street
Oxford
OX2 4JF

Dear Mr Jenks

I am writing to invite you to the presentation of our latest computer business games. As one of our most valued customers, you are, I know, especially interested in this area of the market.

For special customers like yourself we are holding a half-day demonstration of our new games, 'Takeover' and 'Marketing Manager'. This important occasion will be on the morning of 26 March, starting at 10.00 am. The venue will be our new conference centre at head office. Our Chief Designer, Ms Pauline Davi, will open the demonstration.

The timetable for the morning is as follows:

10.00 am   Arrival and coffee
10.30 am   Introduction to new games by Ms Davi
11.00 am   'Hands-on' session and questions
12.00 pm   Buffet lunch

'Takeover' is a game which presents the player with the problems of taking over another company. 'Marketing Manager' involves the player in methods for success in marketing and positive team building. We are very proud of both games; the technology is amazing. I am sure you will learn a lot from both games and find them, at the same time, very enjoyable.

I feel certain that our companies will profit from this presentation.

I look forward to the pleasure of seeing you at the demonstration.

Yours sincerely

Assistant Manager

199 words

Letter-writing situation/task 2: completed letter

Continental Furnishings
4 Rupert Street
Bolton
BL4 6JH

Date of examination

Mr Gerhard Strauss
Conference and Exhibition Centre
Bahnhofstrasse 77
86399 Augsburg
Germany

Dear Mr Strauss

I wish to reserve display space and accommodation for the summer exhibition at the Conference and Exhibition Centre.

This year we shall require 5 display areas. We intend to use 3 of these for a display of living areas and 2 for bedrooms. As well as the 5 display areas we also need an office area for 3 people to work in, and the services of a lighting technician. In addition, will you please reserve for our use accommodation for 2 persons for 2 nights?

As you know we attended last year's exhibition. I am pleased to tell you that we found it most enjoyable. We took several orders at the exhibition and a few more afterwards. This year we are looking for more customers and, we hope, more orders from German firms.

Will you please invoice our Accounts Department direct for the costs of all our reservations?

I look forward to your early confirmation of our booking.

Yours sincerely

Assistant Manager

157 words

Letter-writing situation/task 3: completed letter

Starlight Perfumes
4 Rosewood Square
Chelsea
London
SW4 6BJ

Date of examination

Mrs Liliana Vucic
64 Skadalije
11000 Belgrade
Jugoslavia

Dear Mrs Vucic

It was a great pleasure to meet you recently in London. After talking to you, I left the meeting feeling very enthusiastic. You certainly opened my eyes to the opportunity in my sales job with Starlight Perfumes.

Our firm is seeking new markets in Eastern Europe, and we are looking for a European agent as well. As Chief Buyer for a number of department stores in Eastern Europe, and as an expert in your field, we want you to give us some advice on these matters.

Starlight Perfumes make products to suit all age groups. We have a new perfume ready for the market. This is called 'Eastern Sunset' and we hope it will be one of our best selling perfumes.

I hope very much that you can help us. We admire your great experience in the perfume trade and will welcome any advice you are able to give in finding markets and an agent.

I look forward to receiving your suggestions.

Yours sincerely

Assistant Sales Manager

160 words

Letter-writing situation/task 4: completed letter

Antico Accountants
Arenales 1880
Martinez City
Argentina

Date of examination

The Sales Manager
Alonso Office Supplies
Avellanada 460
San Isidro
Buenos Aires
Argentina

Dear Sir

I very much regret to inform you that the estimate you sent is not correct. I have tried to telephone you about this, but there was no response from your office.

When we asked you to provide an estimate for new office furniture, we made it perfectly clear to you what our requirements were. Your estimate contains the following errors:

- only 3 of the 4 branch offices are included
- only half of the desks we need are included
- the delivery date is wrong.

For each of the 4 offices we require 10 new desks and 20 chairs. We want you to deliver these on 20 September as instructed.

We are disappointed by the poor service you offer. We ask you to give serious attention to the matter. If we do not receive better service, we may cancel this order, which is worth thousands of dollars.

Please confirm by return that everything is now in order.

Yours faithfully

Assistant Accounts and Sales Manager

158 words

Letter-writing situation/task 5: completed letter

Scottish Clothing Company
84 Castle Street
Edinburgh
EB2 6AJ

Date of examination

The Manager
Timpops and Sons
Bismarckstrasse 45–53
42115 Wuppertal
Germany

Dear Madam

I was very sorry to learn that your order has not arrived.

I have looked into the matter of the missing 250 Scottish caps, and I am afraid that it is our fault. I hope you will accept our apologies for the inconvenience.

I checked the files and found the cause of the problem. An error on our computer records showed your account to be in arrears. For this reason the Despatch Department did not send out your order.

I have personally supervised matters now, and the caps will arrive at your warehouse in 3 days. The new delivery date is the 27th of this month. Delivery will be by special carrier.

Our firms have been doing business for 15 years and we are anxious to keep such a highly valued customer. To compensate you we are happy to offer you a further 10% discount on the order. I hope we can continue to do good business.

Please accept our sincere apologies once again.

Yours faithfully

Assistant Sales Manager

162 words

Letter-writing situation/task 6: completed letter

Sparks Electronics
388 Baker Street
London
WC2 2EH

Date of examination

Mrs Helena Papas
Sky TV
Satellite House
Kew Road
London
SW9 4AB

Dear Mrs Papas

Sparks Electronics invite you to be the chief guest and speaker at our '25 Years in Business' celebration, which will be attended by our staff and customers.

Our Chairman, who is a great admirer of you and your chat show, has made you his first choice. His reasons are your great talent and your popularity. He looks forward greatly to your acceptance.

The celebration will be held on the evening of 24 June at the Shangri-la Hotel, starting at 19.30. The timetable is as follows:

19.00	Drinks Reception
20.00	Dinner
21.30	Chairman's Welcome and Guest Speaker
22.15	Dancing

If you accept the invitation, we hope you will speak for about half an hour. The choice of topic is entirely yours. Our guests, mainly electronics experts, will be thrilled to listen. So many have said they enjoy your show. I am sure your speech will be both entertaining and stimulating.

An early reply to this invitation will be welcome.

I hope you will be able to accept our invitation.

Yours sincerely

Assistant Manager

168 words

Letter-writing situation/task 7: completed letter

International Plastics Ltd
84 Church Street
Dundee
DD2 4YS

Date of examination

The Customer Services Manager
Tartanair
Tartanair House
2 The Lapwings
Glasgow
GL1 4BJ

Dear Madam

I wish to register a very strong complaint about my recent flight with your company, Tartanair.

Last Tuesday I flew to Stockholm with Tartanair on flight number TT166 from Glasgow. I was very disappointed indeed with the arrangements.

The trouble started with a 2-hour delay at the airport. On board the plane things steadily got worse. All the in-flight food was cold, and, when I complained to the flight attendant, my comments were ignored. Your flight attendant, who was very rude to me, told me to contact your Customer Services Department. A number of other passengers were also very angry that the food and service were a disgrace.

As a result of all this I very nearly missed an extremely important meeting in Stockholm. I think that some compensation is due, and at this time a further booking from my firm is unlikely.

I hope you will give serious consideration to my request.

Yours faithfully

Manager

154 words

Letter-writing situation/task 8: completed letter

Meridian Carpets Ltd
4 Station Yard
Tewkesbury
TK3 4DN

Date of examination

Mrs Anita Kapaldi
Women Working from Home
The Old Post Office
Brockhampton
Cheltenham
CH4 2BR

Dear Mrs Kapaldi

You will be pleased to hear that our MD has given permission for your group to visit our factory.

The date for your visit will be 26 March starting at 10.00. I have agreed with our MD, Mrs Indira Patel, the following timetable:

10.00	Arrive at reception and coffee
10.30	Talk by Chief Designer, Sandy Tate
11.00	Tour of the factory
12.00	Lunch with our Sales Chief

The numbers for the visit are limited to 15 persons for safety reasons. I am sure you will find the tour interesting. Our staff are used to having visitors. They will enjoy talking to you and showing you their skills.

After the tour, over lunch with the Sales Chief, we will welcome your comments about the factory and its products. You may wish to order some goods after you have seen how they are made.

We all look forward to seeing you on 26 March.

Yours sincerely

Assistant Manager

153 words

Letter-writing situation/task 9: completed letter

Tianhenman Plaza Hotel
44 Wangfujing Avenue
Beijing 10006

Date of examination

The Senior Accountant
Timewise Ltd
68 Union Square
New York 46150
USA

Dear Sir

Thank you very much for your letter concerning Mrs DuPont's invoice.

I have personally checked the invoice, and confirm that all items listed for her 3-night stay are correct. There are no mistakes on the invoice.

The charges for room and service may seem high, but I think you will find that there is a simple explanation for this. The charges are based on Mrs DuPont's requests. These included:

- entertaining guests and clients in her room with drinks and snacks services
- a banquet for 16 persons on her final night
- many telephone calls made from her room.

Please accept our apologies for any distress caused, but we assure you that the amounts are correct. We also assure you that we value your account highly, and try to offer you value-for-money services at all times.

We hope that this explanation is helpful, and look forward to continuing a good business relationship with your company.

Yours faithfully

Accounts Assistant

161 words

Letter-writing situation/task 10: completed letter

Gunter Hopp Fitness and Leisure Club
Königinstrasse 54
11203 Berlin

Date of examination

Ms Natasha Braun
Michelangelostrasse 19
10409 Berlin

Dear Ms Braun

I am very pleased to invite you for interview on 16 November.

The interviews with our manager, Mr Rudi Barenbohm, for the post of Assistant Instructor will start at 14.00. Before the interviews there will be a 1-hour tour of the Gunter Hopp Fitness Centre. On the tour you will meet many of the friendly and helpful staff of this successful club. We therefore ask you to arrive at the Centre in good time for a prompt start at 13.00.

There is a shortlist of 5 for the post. Interviews will be in alphabetical order. Mr Barenbohm wants to see your qualification certificates, so please do not forget to bring these with you.

I enclose a map of the area and details of the arrangements. Please report to reception on arrival. If you have any questions, do not hesitate to contact me.

I look forward to meeting you on 16 November.

Yours sincerely

Administration Assistant

---

152 words

9.2 Memos

Memo-writing situation/task 1

Situation: You work as personal secretary to the new Managing Director of Bentham Ceramics Ltd. The Sales Manager, Carol Dando, is due to retire in a month's time. The local Crossways Hotel has been booked for the occasion, an evening party to which all staff have been invited. There will be a dinner dance and a presentation to Carol by the new MD, Eric Roberts. He has only been in the job for two weeks.

Task: Write a memo to the MD reminding him about the occasion and giving details about:

- Carol's 30 years with Bentham's, starting as office assistant
- Arrangements for the retirement party
- The MD's part in the proceedings.

You may invent any details you think are necessary.

Memo-writing situation/task 2

Situation: You work as the manager of City Taxis in the capital city of your country. Over the last 3 weeks several of your taxis have had traffic accidents. Medical staff at the hospital reported that your drivers were 'too tired to be driving cars'. You have since found out that some of your drivers are working for another taxi firm at night.

Task: Write a memo to all drivers, giving details of your findings. State clearly the firm's policy on safety and working contracts. Give a clear warning of the penalty if the policy is ignored in future.

You may invent any details that you think are necessary.

Memo-writing situation/task 3

Situation: You work as the Assistant Manager of the Osaka Zip Fastener Company in Japan. Recently business has increased by over 100% and the number of staff has doubled. The floor space of your factory is now too small for the workforce and the machinery. The Health and Safety Officer has asked for a review of the situation. He thinks workers are at risk.

Task: Write a memo to the Health and Safety Officer, Mr Kazuyo Akiko. Give your opinion on the situation and your ideas for improvement. A small factory building across the road has just become vacant. Suggest to him that an early meeting with himself and the works supervisor present would be helpful.

You may invent any details you think are necessary.

Memo-writing situation/task 4

Situation: You work in the city of Chang Chun as Assistant Manager of a large electrical showroom. Your area supervisor, Mr T Cheong, has sent you a letter about his last visit. He complains about your staff. He says that they do not take pride in their uniform and that they are not helpful to customers. You know that staff are under pressure, because several staff have not been replaced when they left the firm.

Task: Write a memo to all staff asking for improved performance. Tell them about the letter from Mr Cheong and about what you feel about the present situation.

You may invent any details you think are necessary.

Memo-writing situation/task 5

Situation: You work as a receptionist at Snip and Curl Hair Fashions, which has 6 shops in Los Angeles. Recently you saw an advertisement for a 1-week course in new hair-styling techniques at a nearby college. You feel it would be useful for 2 new trainees who have just joined the staff of Snip and Curl. The 2 girls are showing a lot of promise.

Task: Write a memo to the area staffing supervisor, Gretchen Tomelty. Give details of the course (dates, times, venue, etc) and say why you think it would be helpful to the 2 girls, Janet and Carmel.

You may invent any details you think are necessary.

Memo-writing situation/task 6

Situation: You are employed as Assistant Manager at Sleepytime Beds Ltd. Six new employees are due to start at Sleepytime in a week's time, and the works manager has promised to lead a half-day induction course a few days before they start work. Your MD, Annabella Bergen, usually likes to play a small part in these inductions.

Task: Write a memo to the works manager, Enrico Celli, reminding him of this promise. Say what usually happens on these occasions, and suggest a suitable date, time, and timetable for the half day.

You may invent any details you think are necessary.

Memo-writing situation/task 7

Situation: Your firm, Speedwell Tools Ltd, which makes electrical household tools, has decided to change over to a flexi-hours working system. The hours will be between 6.00 am and 21.00 pm. The 250 workers will be able to choose a weekly pattern of hours. This means a lot of change and staff needs will have to be catered for. A meeting with all senior staff has been arranged to discuss plans.

Task: As Personnel Manager write a memo to the Catering Supervisor, Mrs Tina Carr, to tell her about the meeting, and give her some details of the new proposals. Ask her to send to you, in advance of the meeting, her proposals for dealing with the new hours in her canteen.

You may invent any details that you think are necessary.

Memo-writing situation/task 8

Situation: You are the assistant staffing officer at a large bicycle factory in your country which employs over 100 staff. Yesterday there was a serious fire in the works dining area. This means it will be out of action for 3 weeks. You have hired Meals on Wheels Ltd, a mobile catering firm, to provide a temporary and limited catering service for staff in the car park.

Task: Write a memo to all works supervisors, telling them about the problem with the fire and the provision you have arranged. Stress that workers will not have the wide selection of foods and drink that they usually have. The cost for the 2-week period will be paid for by the firm.

You may invent any details that you think are necessary.

Memo-writing situation/task 9

Situation: You work for a road transport firm, Continental Shipping Ltd, which sends trucks all over Europe. All trucks have 2 drivers for speed of delivery and also for security. Recently thieves have broken into a number of trucks at rest stops. All the incidents have happened at unscheduled rest stops not on the list which you give to drivers. The thefts have cost thousands of pounds in loss of goods and in damage to vehicle locking systems.

Task: Write a memo to all drivers about the problem. Remind them of the firm's policy about rest stops and the rule that vehicles must not be left unattended at any time. Outline the penalty for not working as directed in future.

You may invent any details that you think are necessary.

Memo-writing situation/task 10

Situation: You are employed in the Tourist Information Centre in Hanoi, Vietnam, as the senior receptionist. A number of customers have sent letters of complaint to the Director of Tourism about staff smoking and eating in the main reception and booking areas. The Director has asked you to deal with the situation. She insists that staff must present a better image to customers.

Task: Write a memo to all staff. Mention the letters and the Director's comments to you. Remind the staff of the facilities available to them, and say what you require from them in the future.

You may invent any details that you think are necessary.

Memo-writing situation/task 1: checklist

1 LAYOUT	
To	Mr Eric Roberts/The MD
From	Student's name
Date	Date of examination
Subject	Carol Dando's retirement party

2 CONTENT		
Key points	1 Retirement party	2 For Carol Dando
	3 20 March	4 Crossways Hotel
	5 Dinner/dancing	6 Presentation by Mr Roberts
Additional details	1 30 years with firm	2 All staff invited
Additional invented details	1 Reception 7.30; dinner 8.00	2 Retirement gift a DVD system
	3 Presentation 9.00; dancing at 9.30	4 Plus cheque £500
Sequence of details	1 Retirement party	2 For Carol Dando
	3 20 March	4 Crossways Hotel
	5 All staff invited	6 Dinner and dancing
	7 Presentation by Mr Roberts	8 30 years with firm
	9 Retirement gift a DVD system	10 Plus cheque for £500
	11 Reception 7.30; dinner 8.00	12 Presentation 9.00; dancing 9.30
Opening sentence	Here are the details for Carol Dando's retirement party	
Closing sentence	If I can be of further help, please do not hesitate to ask	

3 STYLE AND TONE		
Writer/addressee relationship	Personal secretary to new MD	Respectful/informative
Purpose of memo	To inform and remind the MD	
Suitable phrases	1 will take place	2 it is the firm's policy
	3 good opportunity to	4 cheerful and reliable worker
	5 short speech praising	6 rest of evening free

Memo-writing situation/task 2: checklist

1 LAYOUT		
To	All drivers	
From	Student's name	
Date	Date of examination	
Subject	Recent traffic accidents	

2 CONTENT		
Key points	1 several traffic accidents	2 last 3 weeks
	3 medical staff reports	4 drivers working at night
	5 company safety policy	6 warning to drivers
Additional details	1 drivers 'too tired'	2 working contracts clear
Additional invented details	1 no serious injuries	2 repair costs high
	3 may make drivers pay	4 suspended or sacked
Sequence of details	1 several traffic accidents	2 last few weeks
	3 no serious injuries	4 medical staff reports
	5 drivers 'too tired'	6 drivers working at night
	7 company safety policy	8 working contracts clear
	9 warning to drivers	10 suspended or fired
	11 repair costs high	12 may make drivers pay
Opening sentence	The number of recent accidents involving drivers is causing concern	
Closing sentence	All drivers are instructed to follow company policy	

3 STYLE AND TONE		
Writer/addressee relationship	Manager to employees	Stern and firm/authoritative
Purpose of memo	To warn and reinforce company policy	
Suitable phrases	1 causing concern	2 medical reports alarming
	3 not observing contracts	4 a serious matter
	5 company will not accept	6 all drivers to obey

Memo-writing situation/task 3: checklist

1 LAYOUT		
To	Mr Kazuyo Akiko or Health and Safety Officer	
From	Student's name	
Date	Date of examination	
Subject	Factory floor space review	

2 CONTENT		
Key points	1 100% increase in business	2 staff doubled
	3 floor space too small	4 H&S Officer review
	5 factory vacant	6 suggest early meeting
Additional details	1 workers at risk	2 works supervisor present
Additional invented details	1 no injuries	2 re-organise production
	3 use vacant factory	4 in-depth look at meeting
Sequence of details	1 H&S Officer review	2 workers at risk
	3 100% increase in business	4 staff doubled
	5 floor space too small	6 no injuries
	7 suggest early meeting	8 in-depth look at meeting
	9 works supervisor present	10 factory vacant
	11 re-organise production	12 use vacant factory
Opening sentence	I am aware of your request for a review of working conditions	
Closing sentence	Please contact me to discuss a suitable date for the meeting	

3 STYLE AND TONE		
Writer/addressee relationship	Assistant Manager to Health and Safety Officer	Friendly/purposeful
Purpose of memo	Response to request for action	
Suitable phrases	1 no cause for alarm	2 I agree fully with . . .
	3 the present situation	4 suitable accommodation
	5 views of works supervisor	6 put forward ideas

Memo-writing situation/task 4: checklist

1 LAYOUT		
To	All staff	
From	Student's name	
Date	Date of examination	
Subject	Staff attitudes to customers	

2 CONTENT		
Key points	1 letter from Mr T Cheong	2 complaints about staff
	3 no pride in uniform	4 not helpful to customers
	5 staff under pressure	6 request improved performance
Additional details	1 last visit	2 staffing difficulties
Additional invented details	1 customers left unattended	2 uniforms dirty/men no ties
	3 staff doing 2 jobs	4 must stop decline
Sequence of details	1 letter from Mr T Cheong	2 last visit
	3 complaints about staff	4 no pride in uniform
	5 uniforms dirty/men no ties	6 not helpful to customers
	7 customers left unattended	8 aware of staffing difficulties
	9 staff under pressure	10 staff doing 2 jobs
	11 must stop decline	12 request improved performance
Opening sentence	I have received a letter from Mr T Cheong, our area supervisor	
Closing sentence	I ask all staff to make a greater effort	

3 STYLE AND TONE		
Writer/addressee relationship	Assistant Manager to staff	Firm but understanding/ Persuasive
Purpose of memo	To enlist support for improved performance	
Suitable phrases	1 he is concerned about	4 staff not replaced
	2 decline in standards	5 must all work together
	3 aware of difficulties	6 I am sure we can succeed

Memo-writing situation/task 5: checklist

1 LAYOUT		
To	Gretchen Tomelty	
From	Student's name	
Date	Date of examination	
Subject	Local college course	

2 CONTENT		
Key points	1 1-week course	2 at local college
	3 2 new trainees	4 Janet and Carmel
	5 girls showing promise	6 benefit from course
Additional details	1 teenage hairstyling techniques	2 St Saviour's College
Additional invented details	1 date and time	2 advertisement in local newspaper
	3 pass on to other staff	4 make them feel confident
Sequence of details	1 1-week course	2 advertisement in local newspaper
	3 teenage hairstyling techniques	4 St Saviour's College
	5 date and time	6 2 new trainees
	7 Janet and Carmel	8 benefit from course
	9 showing promise	10 make them more confident
	11 pass on to other staff	12
Opening sentence	I wish to bring a new course to your attention	
Closing sentence	Please let me know what you think about it	

3 STYLE AND TONE		
Writer/addressee relationship	Receptionist to area supervisor	Friendly/enthusiastic
Purpose of memo	Giving information	
Suitable phrases	1 I have just seen	2 very good reputation
	3 teenage hairstyling	4 pick up skills quickly
	5 get on well with others	6 help us to improve service

Memo-writing situation/task 6: checklist

1 LAYOUT		
To	Enrico Celli	
From	Student's name	
Date	Date of examination	
Subject	Half-day induction course	

2 CONTENT		
Key points	1 half-day induction	2 for 6 new employees
	3 date/time	4 works manager's promise
	5 timetable	6 MD involved
Additional details	1 a few days before start	2
Additional invented details	1 lunch with MD	2 tour the factory
	3 talk about job/questions	4 morning best time
Sequence of details	1 works manager's promise	2 half-day induction
	3 6 new employees	4 few days before start
	5 morning best time	6 date/time
	7 MD involved	8 timetable
	9 tour factory	10 talk about job/questions
	11 lunch with MD	12
Opening sentence	I am sure you have remembered about the induction course next week	
Closing sentence	I hope these arrangements are acceptable	

3 STYLE AND TONE		
Writer/addressee relationship	Assistant Manager to works manager	Friendly/purposeful
Purpose of memo	Remind about induction; suggest timetable	
Suitable phrases	1 may I suggest	2 this fits in well with
	3 occasions work well	4 meet other staff
	5 feel we value them	6 MD likes to find out

Memo-writing situation/task 7: checklist

1 LAYOUT		
To	Tina Carr	
From	Student's name	
Date	Date of examination	
Subject	Change to flexi-hours system	

2 CONTENT		
Key points	1 meeting of senior staff	2 discuss flexi-hours
	3 and changes necessary	4 proposals for canteen
	5 to meet changes	6 before meeting
Additional details	1 6.00 to 21.00 hrs	2 workers choose hours
Additional invented details	1 aim to start in 1 month	2 everything in place
	3 discuss with canteen staff	4 how change will affect service
Sequence of details	1 meeting of senior staff	2 to discuss flexi-hours
	3 and changes necessary	4 6.00 to 21.00 hrs
	5 workers choose hours	6 discuss with canteen staff
	7 how change will affect service	8 proposals of canteen
	9 to meet changes	10 everything in place
	11 aim to start in 1 month	12 proposals before meeting
Opening sentence	I told you last month about the change to a flexi-hours system	
Closing sentence	Please send me your ideas as soon as possible	

3 STYLE AND TONE		
Writer/addressee relationship	Personnel Manager to Catering Supervisor	Informative/business-like
Purpose of memo	Inform about meeting/ask for proposals	
Suitable phrases	1 a big effect on	2 must be sure to
	3 in plenty of time	4 ideas important
	5 essential to have	6 can rely on you

Memo-writing situation/task 8: checklist

1 LAYOUT		
To	All works supervisors	
From	Student's name	
Date	Date of examination	
Subject	Temporary catering arrangements	

2 CONTENT		
Key points	1 works dining area	2 3 weeks out of action
	3 result of fire	4 Meals on Wheels Ltd
	5 supply temporary service	6 firm will pay for everything
Additional details	1 in car park	2 limited choices
Additional invented details	1 fire destroyed whole kitchen	2 covered dining area
	3 introduce dining rota	4 doing all we can
Sequence of details	1 works dining area	2 3 weeks out of action
	3 result of fire	4 fire destroyed whole kitchen
	5 Meals on Wheels Ltd	6 supply temporary service
	7 covered dining area	8 in car park
	9 limited choices	10 introduce dining rota
	11 doing all we can	12 firm will pay for everything
Opening sentence	As you know the works dining area cannot be used	
Closing sentence	I ask you to do all you can to make this work	

3 STYLE AND TONE		
Writer/addressee relationship	Assistant staffing officer to works supervisors	Friendly/informative
Purpose of memo	Inform and enlist support	
Suitable phrases	1 I am afraid that	2 to repair and re-equip
	3 pleased to tell you	4 experienced and reliable firm
	5 please make clear	6 workers will approve

Memo-writing situation/task 9: checklist

1 LAYOUT		
To	All drivers	
From	Student's name	
Date	Date of examination	
Subject	Security policy reminder	

2 CONTENT		
Key points	1 recent truck break-ins	2 costing £1,000s
	3 despite 2-driver system	4 unauthorised rest stops
	5 company policy ignored	6 warning of penalty
Additional details	1 stolen goods/vehicle damage	2 authorised rest stops/ guarding vehicles
Additional invented details	1 vehicles out of use	2 2-driver system must operate
	3 lack of care by drivers	4 drivers risk being fired
Sequence of details	1 company policy not followed	2 using unauthorised rest stops
	3 recent truck break-ins	4 costing £1,000s
	5 stolen goods/damage to vehicles	6 vehicles out of use
	7 despite 2-driver system	8 lack of care by drivers
	9 authorised rest stops/ guarding vehicles	10 2-driver system must operate
	11 warning of penalty	12 drivers face dismissal
Opening sentence	The company policy on vehicle security is not being followed by drivers	
Closing sentence	I expect a big effort from all drivers to improve vehicle security	

3 STYLE AND TONE		
Writer/addressee relationship	Senior member of staff to drivers	Firm/factual
Purpose of memo	Reprimand/instruct/warn	
Suitable phrases	1 not following regulations	2 profits have gone down
	3 a lot of inconvenience	4 policy must be followed
	5 will not be accepted	6 risk being fired

Memo-writing situation/task 10: checklist

1 LAYOUT		
To	All staff	
From	Student's name	
Date	Date of examination	
Subject	Smoking and eating in public areas	
2 CONTENT		
Key points	1 letters of complaint	2 staff smoking and eating
	3 reception/booking areas	4 number of facilities
	5 customers important	6 better image needed
Additional details	1 Director of Tourism	2 deal with situation
Additional invented details	1 while using telephone	2 or talking to customers
	3 Director shocked	4 damage to national image
Sequence of details	1 Director of Tourism	2 letters of complaint
	3 staff smoking and eating	4 reception/booking areas
	5 while using telephone	6 talking to customers
	7 Director shocked	8 deal with situation
	9 facilities available	10 customers important
	11 damage to national image	12 better image needed
Opening sentence	The Director of Tourism is not happy with our service	
Closing sentence	It is up to us all to make these things happen – now!	
3 STYLE AND TONE		
Writer/addressee relationship	Senior receptionist to staff	Friendly but firm
Purpose of memo	Set standards in workplace	
Suitable phrases	1 giving a poor impression	2 customers expect better
	3 cannot be ignored	4 enough private areas
	5 make a greater effort	6 immediate steps

MEMO-WRITING	CHECKLIST FOR SITUATION/TASK	
1 LAYOUT		
To		
From		
Date		
Subject		
2 CONTENT		
Key points	1	2
	3	4
	5	6
Additional details	1	2
	3	4
Additional invented details	1	2
	3	4
Sequence of details	1	2
	3	4
	5	6
	7	8
	9	10
	11	12
Opening sentence		
Closing sentence		
3 STYLE AND TONE		
Writer/addressee relationship		
Purpose of memo		
Suitable phrases	1	2
	3	4
	5	6

Memorandum I

TO   Mr Eric Roberts OR The MD

FROM   Student's name

DATE   Date of examination

SUBJECT   Carol Dando's retirement party

Here are the details for Carol Dando's retirement party. This will take place on 20 March at the Crossways Hotel, starting at 7.30 pm.

It is the firm's policy to invite all staff to these social events. It is a good opportunity for people to meet and chat. There will be a reception followed by dinner and dancing for everyone.

We would like you, of course, to make the presentation to Carol. She has been a cheerful and reliable worker in the firm for 30 years. Her leaving present is a DVD system, plus a cheque for £500. A short speech praising her work for the firm will be very nice. The rest of the evening is free for dancing and enjoying ourselves.

The timetable for the evening is as follows:

7.30 pm   Reception
8.00 pm   Dinner
9.00 pm   Presentation
9.30 pm   Dancing

If I can be of further help, please do not hesitate to ask.

154 words

Memorandum 2

TO	All drivers
FROM	Student's name
DATE	Date of examination
SUBJECT	Recent traffic accidents

The number of traffic accidents involving drivers is causing concern. There have been several accidents in the last 3 weeks involving our cars. Luckily there have been no serious injuries, but the medical staff's reports from the hospital are alarming. They say drivers are 'too tired' to drive.

I have found out that this is because some drivers are not observing their contracts. They are going out at night working for another firm. This is a very serious matter. The company safety policy does not allow drivers to take on other work. This is known by every driver, as your work contracts make perfectly clear.

Drivers are warned that the company will not accept any breaking of the rules. All drivers must obey the company safety policy, or face being suspended or sacked.

The repair costs to vehicles are high, and in future we may make drivers pay these costs themselves.

All drivers are instructed to follow company policy.

159 words

Memorandum 3

TO	Mr Kazuyo Akiko or Health and Safety Officer
FROM	Student's name
DATE	Date of examination
SUBJECT	Factory floor space review

I am aware of your request for a review of working conditions. You say workers may be at risk because the floor space is too small. This has happened because we have increased business by 100% and have doubled our staff.

I do not feel that there is any call for alarm at present, because there have been no injuries to workers.

I agree fully with you that the present situation is unsatisfactory. I suggest we hold an early meeting to take an in-depth look. I think the works supervisor should be present. His views are most important.

There is a vacant factory across the road from our site. This can probably provide suitable accommodation. Perhaps we can re-organise production and use the vacant building.

I shall be most grateful if you will put forward any ideas you have.

Please contact me to discuss a suitable date for the meeting.

150 words

Memorandum 4

TO	All staff
FROM	Student's name
DATE	Date of examination
SUBJECT	Staff attitudes to customers

I have just received a letter from the area supervisor, Mr T Cheong. The letter is about his last visit and in the letter he makes several complaints about the staff here. He is concerned about a decline in personal standards. He says staff take no pride in their uniform, which is often dirty. He says the men do not wear ties. He also says that staff are not helpful to customers and that the customers are often left unattended.

I am aware of the difficulties that we have at present. We have not received replacements for people who have recently left, and everyone is under pressure. I know that some staff are doing two jobs.

We must do our best to stop the decline. I am sure we can succeed if we all work together to improve our service to customers.

I ask all staff to make a greater effort.

151 words

Memorandum 5

TO	Gretchen Tomelty
FROM	Student's name
DATE	Date of examination
SUBJECT	Local college course

I wish to bring a new course to your attention. I have just seen in the local newspaper an advertisement for a 1-week course in teenage hairstyling techniques. This is going to be held at the local St Saviour's College. The course takes place in 2 weeks' time and will be held in normal working hours. I understand that St Saviour's College has a very good reputation.

I am sure our 2 new trainees, Janet and Carol, will benefit a lot from such a course. They both pick up skills quickly and they certainly get on well with the other staff. They are definitely showing promise and I am sure this course will make them feel more confident. They can also pass on the things they learn to other staff.

I am sure it will help us to improve our service to customers.

Please let me know what you think about it.

153 words

Memorandum 6

TO	Enrico Celli
FROM	Student's name
DATE	Date of examination
SUBJECT	Half-day induction course

I am sure you have remembered about the induction course next week. You made a promise to lead the course for our 6 new employees a few days before they start work for us.

I have arranged for the course to be on the 26th of this month. May I suggest that we hold it in the morning starting at 10.00 am? This fits in well with the MD who always likes to be involved in these activities. These occasions work well.

I suggest a timetable as follows:

10.00   Arrival of the new employees.
10.15   A tour of the factory with yourself.
11.30   Opportunity to talk about the job and ask questions.
12.00   Lunch with the MD.

The tour allows them to meet and talk with other staff. Lunch with the MD makes employees feel that we value them, and the MD likes to find out about them for herself.

I hope these arrangements are acceptable.

154 words

Memorandum 7

TO	Tina Carr (Catering Supervisor)
FROM	Student's name
DATE	Date of examination
SUBJECT	Change to flexi-hours working

I told you last month about the change to a flexi-hours system.

I have arranged a meeting of senior staff to discuss the flexi-hours system and the changes we shall need to make. It will have a big effect on how we operate.

The new working hours will be from 6.00 am until 21.00 pm and workers will be able to choose their hours.

You must be sure to discuss this with your canteen staff in plenty of time. Their ideas are most important. We need to know how the changes will affect your services. It is essential to have details of your proposals to meet the changes in working hours.

We want to have everything in place, and we aim to start the new system in a month's time.

I need your proposals before the meeting. I am sure I can rely on you.

Please send me your ideas as soon as possible.

151 words

Memorandum 8

TO	All works supervisors
FROM	Student's name
DATE	Date of examination
SUBJECT	Temporary catering arrangements

As you know the works dining area cannot be used. I am afraid it will be out of action for 3 weeks because of the recent fire. The fire destroyed the whole kitchen area and it will take that time to repair and re-equip.

I am pleased to tell you that I have made arrangements with Meals on Wheels Ltd to supply a temporary catering service. They are an experienced and reliable firm, and they will provide a covered area for dining in the works car park.

Please make it clear to workers that the choice of food will be limited, and that we shall need to operate a rota for dining.

I am sure that workers will approve the arrangements and see that we are doing all we can.

The firm will pay for everything, including the food.

I ask you to do all you can to make this work.

152 words

Memorandum 9

TO	All drivers
FROM	Student's name
DATE	Date of examination
SUBJECT	Security policy reminder

The company policy on vehicle security is not being followed by drivers. I am fully aware that many drivers are choosing to ignore the strict regulations and are using unauthorised rest stops when taking their breaks. This is not allowed.

The recent truck break-ins at these places are costing the company thousands of pounds. Goods are stolen and the vehicles are being damaged in the process. The damage means that they are out of use. Company profits have gone down and the incidents themselves cause a lot of inconvenience.

The policy on vehicle security must be followed. The 2-driver system must operate and, in future, any examples of carelessness by drivers will not be accepted. Only authorised rest stops must be used and vehicles must be guarded at all times.

Drivers who do not obey these instructions run the risk of being sacked.

I expect a big effort from all drivers to improve vehicle security.

154 words

Memorandum 10

TO	All staff
FROM	Student's name
DATE	Date of examination
SUBJECT	Smoking and eating in public areas

The Director of Tourism is not happy with our service. He has received some letters of complaint from customers. These complaints state that members of staff are giving a very poor impression of our department by smoking and eating in the booking and reception areas. This is happening when they are using the telephone or talking to customers.

The Director is shocked and he has asked me personally to deal with the situation. Customers who are visiting our department can expect better treatment than this.

We have a large number of facilities in private areas of the centre which can be used for eating and smoking.

I think that we must all make a greater effort to make customers feel more important. We are damaging our national image, and we must take immediate steps to achieve a better image.

It is up to us all to make these things happen – now!

152 words

10

Past examination questions and Chief Examiners' reports

This chapter contains the questions from the papers for:

- English for Business First Level Series 3 1999

- English for Business First Level Series 4 1999.

You will find this chapter useful, if you study it carefully. The Chief Examiners' reports have been made simpler to help you understand them. They comment on the work of candidates for each examination and offer suggestions on how to answer the questions well. They also offer tips on what not to do. Try to answer the questions before you consult the model answers in Appendix 2.

10.1 Series 3 1999 questions and Chief Examiner's report

General comments

There was a large entry for this series and many candidates gained marks in either the credit or distinction grades. It is always good to see students gaining the higher grades and producing answers which show their skills in writing and understanding. Many candidates wrote a memo with the correct tone and style for the task, and included all the relevant information. The correct tone and style are needed to achieve the higher grades. The skills of memo-writing continue to improve.

The revised rubrics for Questions 2 and 3 are working well. More candidates are now following the instructions carefully for Questions 2 and 3. The result is that their answers can be fully rewarded. Many more candidates are now gaining maximum marks on these questions.

All the information needed for correct and appropriate answers is on the paper and in the question situations and tasks. It is still important to remind students that they should see the examination as an *opportunity* to display their skills in Business English; this is more positive than seeing it as a *test*. The board wants students to be successful and seeing the examination in this way will help students like yourself by boosting your confidence.

More detailed comment and guidance can be found in the individual question reports.

QUESTION 1: A MEMO

Situation: Your department is responsible for the ordering and issuing of stationery supplies to employees in your organisation. The Accounts Manager has recently pointed out the rising costs of stationery used. He suspects that employees are being wasteful, and wants you to take some action to reduce the amounts.

Task: **Write a memo** to all company staff. Give details of the Accounts Manager's complaint, and stress the need for economy and careful use of stationery items You need to tell them that you will shortly discuss with other department heads the introduction of new guidelines for stationery requisition.

Lay out your answer as a **memo** in the space below. Make up any necessary details.

(30 marks)

MEMORANDUM

TO

FROM

DATE

SUBJECT

QUESTION 1 CONTINUED

You may continue writing here.

The task for candidates was to write a memo suitable for distribution to all staff about the need to use stationery supplies with care and not wastefully. A complaint from the Accounts Manager had been received. Candidates needed to write in a way to persuade staff to co-operate with the request. The memo must not be a threat to the staff. The Examiner rewarded candidates who produced a logically planned memo, which was written in a non-threatening tone and style. Whilst candidates could frame their own approach to the task, the following elements were expected for a higher grade:

- suitable opening and closing sentences.
- details of the Account Manager's complaint.
- instructions for immediate careful use of stationery.
- mention of new guidelines for saving stationery.

The format required was that of a standard memo within the usual framework printed on the answer paper. A memo of 150–200 words was the correct length to deal with the subject and to gain the higher grades.

Many candidates responded well to the task and produced well composed memos. They wrote in a business-like style and tone, and included all the relevant information. Some candidates wrote memos that were too short. This meant that important points were missing and often the wrong tone was used. These memos seemed rude and threatening to the staff. Memos are supposed to be 'crisper' than letters, but candidates must not write a memo that is too short to *do the job*. More than anything a short memo shows that the candidate has not planned the answer carefully.

Helpful hints for candidates

- Read carefully and make notes on precisely what you are asked to do.
- Draft a plan for your memo.
- Keep sentences simple and to the point.
- Add your own details when you draft the plan.
- Decide what the relationship is between writer and the person(s) the memo is written to (the addressee). This affects the style and tone of the memo.
- Check spelling and grammar to avoid losing marks.
- Ask yourself – does the memo *do the job*? Is it clear and accurate?

A model answer for the question is provided in Appendix 2, page 205, but you may find the following example of a memo for this question useful. The example shows how the wrong length, and the wrong tone, make a memo unsuitable, even if the actual content is fairly accurate. The bold type is the Examiner's.

Example

TO   All company staff

FROM   Head of stationery supplies

DATE   12/6/99

SUBJECT   **Being wasteful**

You may not know this but the Accounts Manager has just informed me that there is a rising cost in the stationery that is being used in our department. **I am not pointing fingers at any one person** but I would tell you all that it is unacceptable to be wasteful with any of our goods as it does cost the company money that can be used for other things. The latest figures have forced me to get together with the heads of other departments to introduce new guidelines for the use of stationery requisitions. This is a serious matter and **I don't want to have to write another memo about this subject.**

Points to note here include:

- The memo is short.
- The memo contains phrases which are abrupt.
- The memo threatens the reader (staff).
- The memo does not encourage staff support.
- The memo does not suit the purpose at all.

This example was given an overall mark of 11 out of 30.

QUESTION 2: TRUE-OR-FALSE QUESTIONS

Situation: Your company is considering a healthcare package for all employees and you have been asked to look at a number of options.

Task: Read the information on Tip-Top Health Insurance on the page opposite, then say whether the following statements are **TRUE** or **FALSE**. Then quote the **words or phrase** that supports your answer. Do not write more than 6 words for each answer. You will lose marks for irrelevant information.

Write your answers on the lines marked A.

1 Only rich people can afford private healthcare.

A _____

2 Every sixth year with Tip-Top is automatically free.

A _____

3 Tip-Top's budget policy covers all medical expenses.

A _____

4 Tip-Top is Britain's oldest health insurance company.

A _____

5 A recent poll showed Tip-Top to be the equal of other companies.

A _____

6 With Tip-Top you may not get quick treatment or the doctor you want.

A _____

7 At Tip-Top hospitals friends can come and see you when they like within reason.

A _____

8 Tip-Top insurance does not apply outside your home country.

A _____

9 The Gold Scheme has no equal, but Silver is the scheme chosen most often.

A _____

10 To find out about an illness you must visit a hospital or see a doctor.

A _____

(30 marks)

QUESTION 2 CONTINUED

TIP-TOP HEALTH INSURANCE

If any member of your organisation needed urgent medical treatment, do you know what would happen? Would you be sure of getting treatment for your employee as fast as you would like, or would you lose time and production through a long absence from work?

With the benefit of Tip-Top Health Insurance you can be certain of fast, first-class treatment at a hospital of your choice. And you can also choose the doctor you want. Your employee would have a comfortable private room. Friends and family would be able to visit more freely, because the visiting hours in our group of hospitals are more flexible and convenient.

Personal private healthcare is now within the reach of all people, with a wide choice of schemes and premiums to pay. And nobody has done more to bring this about than Tip-Top. We help so many people and companies. Tip-Top Health Insurance is not only Britain's largest healthcare insurer; it has also been established the longest with schemes that start from as little as £1.25 a week depending on the level of care you want. What's more, every sixth year is FREE after 5 claim-free years.

Tip-Top has won numerous awards. A recent poll placed Tip-Top ahead of all its leading competitors in the health insurance service. Just look at the benefits again:

Accommodation and care in private hospitals
Specialist fees paid for consultations and treatment
Nursing at home if needed
Worldwide cover when you travel overseas.

Tip-Top is aware that when illness strikes, finding out more about a problem can help. So we have introduced our Health Line Information Service. You can call at any time to find out about over 450 health-related topics.

So why not consider our 3 schemes NOW?

GOLD
The very best in private health insurance, providing high levels of benefit to cover your healthcare needs.

SILVER
Tip-Top's most popular health insurance scheme also giving a wide range of benefits for very affordable subscriptions.

BRONZE
Our budget policy that covers all in-patient hospital costs.

Interested? Telephone now for our free brochure. Our lines are open 24 hours a day on 0800 777 666.

Candidates were asked to read a passage about possible healthcare providers for their company. They were then asked to decide whether 10 statements related to the information in the passage were **true** or **false**. They were then asked to quote up to 6 words from the passage to support their answer.

There were many candidates who answered correctly in the first part and chose their support material with care. The new rubric again helped a great many candidates to answer correctly and limit their support words to 6 per answer. Candidates must do this or they will lose marks.

Some candidates did not supply any support material when they said a statement was **true**. *All* answers must have support material (maximum 6 words) to gain full marks.

Some candidates failed to **quote** from the passage. '**Quote**' means '*write words exactly as they appear*'. The support material must be an accurate quotation from the passage. The 6 words quoted need not be 6 consecutive words. Most support answers consist of two specific parts, each part from a different section of the passage.

Helpful hints for candidates

- Read the passage carefully and thoroughly.
- Make sure you understand the passage and the statements.
- Supply support quotation for all answers.
- Limit your support quotation to 6 words only.

The model answer for this question is in Appendix 2, page 206.

QUESTION 3: SHORT-ANSWER QUESTIONS

Situation: You have been asked to write a report on the recent in-service training of some of your staff.

Task: Study the information in the Staff Training Record, then answer the questions below. Keep your answers very short. Figures and/or single word answers are acceptable.

ANSWERS

1 How many staff have had a total of 10 days' training?

2 Which department received no training for 2 consecutive years?

3 Who has had more training, Tony Hart or Tony Harrison?

4 Who had one day less training than Zuber Patel?

5 Have both people in Management received training every year?

6 In which year did Rikki Helsing receive most training?

7 In 1996 how many people received only a single day's training?

8 Did Stuart Simpson miss training between 1994 and 1997?

9 Which of Stuart Simpson's colleagues in Workshop had the most training in 1997?

10 In which year did Val Booth receive more than 3 days' training?

11 How many staff have had less training than Jill Pike?

12 In Sales, who had no training in 1994?

13 To which department does the person with most training overall belong?

14 Which department has received the least training?

15 Did the Sales Department receive more training in 1995 or 1997?

16 How many employees have had less training than Paul Fox?

17 In 1995 how many employees had more than one day's training?

18 Who received the most training in 1997 and 1996?

19 For how many years did Graham Chesters receive less than 2 days' training?

20 In which year was the least training taken overall?

(20 marks)

QUESTION 3 CONTINUED

STAFF TRAINING RECORD (Days each year)

	1998	1997	1996	1995	1994	TOTAL
SALES						
Tony Hart	3	1	1	3	6	14
Jill Pike	0	2	2	2	4	10
May Wilson	6	3	3	1	0	13
Duncan Kyle	5	5	3	1	3	17
Val Booth	4	0	1	2	3	10
WAREHOUSE						
Mel Bailey	3	0	0	2	0	5
Graham Chesters	2	0	0	1	1	4
WORKSHOP						
Heidi Heimstadt	4	0	0	1	2	7
Stuart Simpson	2	2	1	2	5	12
Anna Socic	2	3	3	3	0	11
CLERICAL						
Tony Harrison	4	4	0	1	4	13
Norma Wood	3	6	6	0	5	20
Rikki Helsing	2	4	6	1	1	14
Zuber Patel	6	5	2	3	5	21
MANAGEMENT						
Paul Fox	3	3	1	0	3	10
Jerri Casals	4	0	4	3	2	13
TOTALS	53	38	33	26	44	194

Candidates were asked to study a Staff Training Record before answering a series of questions about the information in the chart. Most candidates scored very high marks. The new rubric guided candidates to answer in a single word, or with a name, or in figures. If a name is the correct answer, then the full name (e.g. John Smith) must be written.

Helpful hints for candidates

- Read the chart carefully before you start to attempt to answer the questions.

- As instructed, answer with a single word, or a name, or in figures.

- Check your answers carefully. Sometimes candidates miss out a line, or write on the wrong line.

- Make sure that you read carefully any footnotes or asterisks connected to the chart if they appear. (There is none on this particular question.)

The model answer for this question is in Appendix 2, page 206.

QUESTION 4: A CHART

Situation: You are visiting Suncare Ltd. Your firm is considering placing a large order with them and your manager has asked you to check the quality of their organisation.

Task: Use the information below (which is part of your conversation with Peter Corrie, the Joint Managing Director of Suncare Ltd) and **complete the Staffing Organisation Chart printed on the page opposite.**

'Well, as you can see, there are two of us at the top, myself and Jane Kovak. I look after the Sales and Marketing sides, as well as Production Research. All the Staff Training, Accounts and Personnel issues are handled by Jane. There's a manager for each of the six areas – Ivan Korda does Sales, and his Marketing colleague is Denise Woodley. Production Research is in the hands of Miss Tanya Lowe – we only appointed her last week.

We should have an assistant for each departmental area, but we're one short at present. Craig Loftus is in Sales and Siobhan McKenna is in Production Research. We hope to replace Helen Sparks in Marketing early next week.

Jane and I also have a Personal Assistant each; mine is Ursula Stein, and Julie Stableford helps Jane.

Jane's three managers are Ben Schweik in Training, Carmen Velasquez in Accounts, and, let me think ... oh yes, Chris Penn is the third. Their assistants are Paul Robey (for Carmen), Danielle Lefevre in Personnel, and Dan Lyons.

Both teams, Jane's and mine, have the services of two Secretarial Assistants to each team. Linda Fellows works for my team, and her sister Karen for Jane's. They share the work with Tina Glass and Ava Merrill. Ava completes my team.'

Complete the Chart.

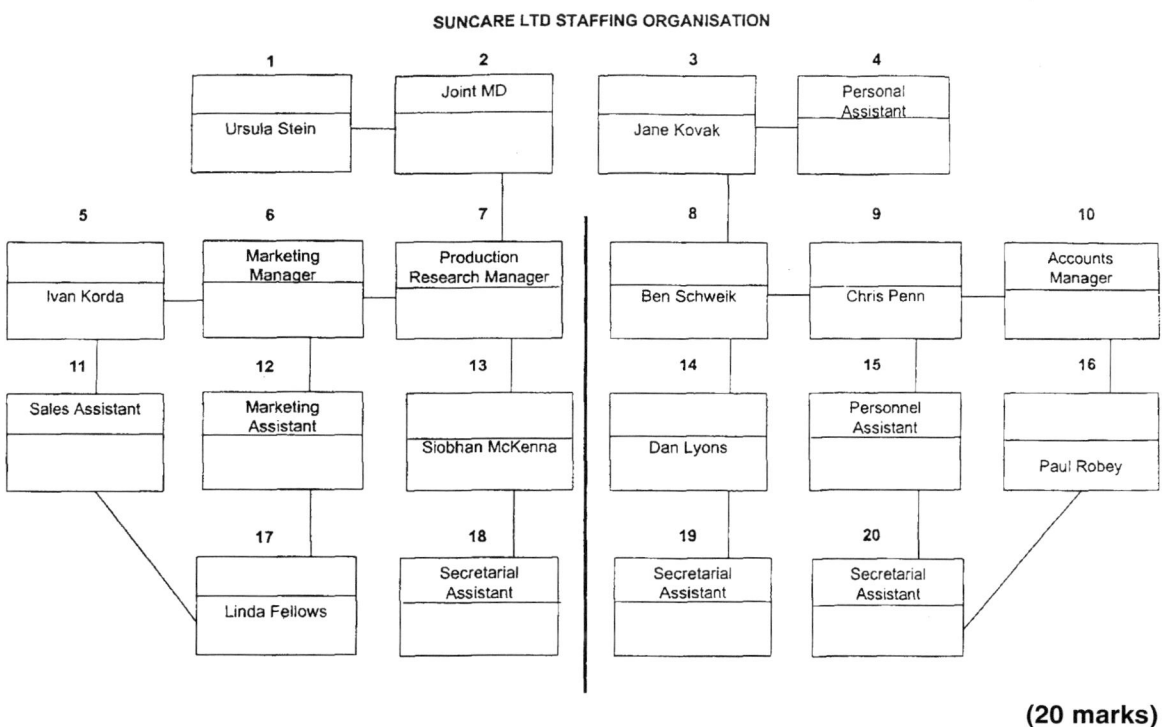

SUNCARE LTD STAFFING ORGANISATION

(20 marks)

Candidates were asked to complete a Staffing Organisation Chart. The information for this was in the form of comments by a Managing Director. The comments explained:

- which staff performed which tasks
- and who each member of staff reported to.

This was a hard question. The better candidates performed well, but there were many candidates who had problems with the question. This was partly caused by not reading the information carefully enough. There were clues in the completed boxes, but many did not read carefully, or did not realise how important these clues were. Many candidates did not 'mirror' exactly the similar job titles; for instance, box 13 should be labelled 'Production Research Assistant'. This is because box 7 above is labelled 'Production Research Manager' and all the Assistant boxes carry the full department name. Thus we have in box 6 'Marketing Manager' and in box 12 'Marketing Assistant'. For this reason the answer 'Production Assistant' for box 13 is not correct. The correct answer must be 'Production Research Assistant'.

Many candidates did not place Ava Merrill in box 18, but the MD's comments clearly say: '**Ava completes my team**'.

Two names could go in either box 19 or box 20.

Your success in this type of exercise depends on very careful reading. You need to trace the path for each team accurately. The information already in some boxes will help you to do this more easily. Just keep calm and work logically from one clue to the next.

The model answer for this question is in Appendix 2, page 207.

10.2 Series 4 1999 questions and Chief Examiner's report

General comments

There was again a large entry for the examination and many candidates gained marks in the credit or distinction grades. Weaker candidates continue, of course, to present themselves with varying degrees of success and failure. There is no substitute for continued practice and for careful reading of questions.

There were many very well-written letters. The new-style rubrics for questions 2 and 3 continue to help candidates to answer accurately, and appropriately. Many more candidates are now gaining high or full marks on these questions.

All the information needed for successful answers is on the paper and in the question situations. It is still important to remind students that they should see the examination as an *opportunity* to display their skills in Business English rather than as a *test*. This approach will assist students by boosting confidence in their own ability.

There is more detailed comment and guidance in the individual question reports.

QUESTION 1: A BUSINESS LETTER

Situation: You work as an administrative assistant at the Acme Vacuum Cleaner Company, whose address is Fall Birch Road, Henbury, Gloucester GL2 5ER. The company employs over 150 workers. The employees' car park, which takes over 100 cars, is shortly to be resurfaced. The work will take 2 weeks to complete, and you need to find temporary car-parking space for your workers. The James North High School, which is on holiday for 3 weeks at the time of the resurfacing work, is just across from the factory and has ample parking space for your needs. Your company recruits regularly from the school. The Headteacher has said she is happy to help you, but has asked you to write to the District Office for official permission.

Task: **Write a suitable letter** to the District Education Officer, Ms Janet Duxbury, whose address is Atlas House, The Wellsprings, Henbury, Gloucester GL1 3LD. Ask for permission to use the car park of the school for 2 weeks.

Lay out your answer as a **business letter** in the space below. Make up any necessary details.

QUESTION 1 CONTINUED

You may continue writing here.

(30 marks)

The task for candidates was to write a letter to the District Education Officer to request permission to use the car park of a school for a 2-week period. This requires a formal business letter using the information about time, place, reasons, etc, given in the rubric.

The format required was that of a standard letter with the usual business layout. A letter of 150–200 words was sufficient to deal with the subject and to gain the higher grades.

Many candidates responded well to the task and produced well composed letters which effectively established the situation and approached the task in a way which would have elicited a favourable response from the recipient. Most candidates produced a letter of the required length and thereby dealt fully with the task. Candidates who wrote shorter letters often missed out vital points of information relevant to the task. Good candidates wrote with a confident touch, explaining the school's relationship with the factory and the important fact that the Headteacher was fully supportive of the request.

The 'trap', if it can be called such, since candidates only needed to read with care to grasp the letter's purpose and its destination, was to include both the Headteacher and the District Education Officer. Many weaker candidates confused the two people and wrote to the wrong person.

Helpful hints for candidates

- Read carefully and make notes on precisely what you are asked to do.
- Decide on the layout, the appropriate salutation and the complimentary close.
- Draft a plan for your letter.
- Add your own details when you draft the plan.
- Keep your sentences simple and to the point.
- Make sure your letter 'flows' – ie has a logical sequence.
- Check spellings and grammar to avoid losing marks unnecessarily.
- Ask yourself – does the letter do the job? Is it clear and accurate?

A model answer for this question is provided in Appendix 2, page 208. Teachers and candidates should remind themselves, however, that a model answer is only *one* way of approaching the task. There is an infinite number of alternatives which would gain equally high marks.

QUESTION 2: TRUE-OR-FALSE QUESTIONS

Situation: Your kitchenware company is considering new ways of advertising locally to increase sales.

Task: Read the information on 'House to House Leaflets' on the page opposite, then say whether the following statements are **TRUE** or **FALSE**. Then write down only the **word** or **phrase** that supports your answer. Do NOT write more than 6 words for each answer. You will lose marks if you write more than 6 supporting words.

Write your answers on the lines marked A.

1   PC Computer Software and Carfax Home Help have reduced their staff.

A   _____

2   House to House claims that it can improve a firm's local advertising.

A   _____

3   Clients of House to House pay more for the 'check-back system'.

A   _____

4   House to House offers only one service – leaflet distribution.

A   _____

5   You can receive free artwork if you order 3,000 copies in January 2000.

A   _____

6   House to House has less than 100 branches, all in the south-east of England.

A   _____

7   Teenagers, who have received basic training, deliver the leaflets for House to House.

A   _____

8   House to House has traded for only 6 years.

A   _____

9   You can have leaflets delivered on Sundays if you prefer.

A   _____

10   House to House leaflet printing takes longer than a day.

A   _____

(30 marks)

QUESTION 2 CONTINUED

HOUSE TO HOUSE LEAFLETS

Let HOUSE TO HOUSE help your business to find new customers!

With over 150 branches we specialise in fast, efficient leaflet distribution and use highly-trained staff.

We can make your local advertising more effective – cheaper than newspaper advertisements and cheaper than local TV advertising.

We can deliver your message to every household in your area – *or any other area. As often as you like AND as soon as you like. Just give us a call.*

House to House has been established for over 15 years.

We are the proven experts in:

leaflet design (24 hour service)
leaflet printing (48 hour service)
leaflet distribution (7 days a week)

and ALL at low, low prices. Just look at the comments from 2 of our regular customers.

'We made the right choice coming to you. Since our Spring leaflet campaign our sales enquiries have risen by 100%. The phone never stops, and we've had to employ another telephone receptionist to keep pace with demand. Thanks.' *Carfax Home Help*	'We have appointed extra sales staff because business has boomed. House to House deserves a medal. We're already planning our next leaflet – and we know who will deliver them – YOU! Thank you for everything. *PC Computer Software*

We offer a safe, reliable service, with all staff over 21 years of age.

Our check-back system on delivery offers you a further guarantee of reliability AT NO EXTRA COST, and just think, with a delivery team of 100 people, we can 'post' your leaflet to 20,000 houses in a single day.

Whatever your trade is, come and talk to us. Our expert staff can even help you with leaflet design. Indeed, artwork is FREE when you order 5,000 copies.**

We operate throughout the UK.

Just telephone us on FREEPHONE 0800-373635 for information about your nearest branch – AND START SELLING MORE!

** special offer runs until 20 December 1999

Candidates were asked to read a passage about the delivery of leaflets house to house. They were then asked whether each of 10 statements related to the information in the passage was **true** or **false**. They were then asked to **quote** no more than 6 words from the passage to support their answer. The new rubric continues to help more candidates to answer correctly and to limit their support material to 6 words per answer. This must be done for full marks.

Some candidates did not supply support material for statements they said were **true**. All answers must have support material, limited to a maximum of 6 words.

Some candidates still fail to **quote** accurately from the passage. '**Quote**' means to write down the words exactly as they appear in the passage. The support material must be accurately quoted for full marks. The 6 words quoted need not be 6 consecutive words; most support answers consist of two parts. In some answers two separate phrases from different parts of the passage form the correct answer.

Helpful hints for candidates

- Read the passage carefully and thoroughly.
- Make sure you understand the passage and the statements.
- Supply support quotation for all answers, maximum 6 words per answer.

The model answer for this question is in Appendix 2, page 209.

QUESTION 3: SHORT-ANSWER QUESTIONS

Situation: Your company is planning to set up a number of regional distribution bases in the UK.

Task: Study the information on the chart, then answer the questions below. Your answers need not be more than 2 words or a figure.

ANSWERS

1   How many sites in the Midlands are within 10 miles of the motorway?

2   How many sites in Wales have room for expansion?

3   How many regions have a site cost of more than £100 per square metre?

4   Which region is served by the port of Liverpool?

5   Which region has the most sites with room for expansion?

6   Are relocation grants available in the London region?

7   Has Scotland more sites available than the South East?

8   How many sites are served by the port of Belfast?

9   Apart from London, how many regions do not offer relocation grants?

10   How many regions have no sites with room for expansion?

11   Does the port of Hull serve the Scottish sites?

12   Which costs more per square metre, a site in Scotland or a site in the North West?

13   Which port serves the greatest number of sites?

14   Which region has the most sites more than 10 miles from a motorway?

15   Which region offers a relocation grant and is cheapest per square metre?

16   Which port serves the region with the highest cost per square metre?

17   In which region do all the sites have room for expansion?

18   How many regions have more sites available than Wales?

19   How many regions have fewer than 10 sites with room for expansion?

20   Has Northern Ireland fewer sites than any other region?

(20 marks)

INFORMATION ON DISTRIBUTION BASES

REGION	£ per square metre	Number of Suitable Sites in Region	Number of Sites with Room for Expansion	Number of Sites within 10 Miles of a Motorway	Nearest Port	Relocation Grants Available
South East	120	12	5	9	Dover	Yes
South West	100	6	6	3	Plymouth	Yes
London	160	4	0	4	London	No
Midlands	155	15	9	11	Hull	No
North West	105	18	9	11	Liverpool	Yes
North East	85	22	18	13	Newcastle	Yes
Scotland	110	16	12	5	Glasgow	No
Wales	80	8	7	2	Cardiff	Yes
Northern Ireland	75	3	0	1	Belfast	No

Candidates were asked to study a chart of suitable regional distribution bases for their company. They had to supply answers to a series of questions about the information in the chart. Most candidates scored very high marks. The new rubric again guided candidates to answer by writing a single word, or a name, or in figures. An increased number of candidates gained full marks.

Helpful hints for candidates

- Read the chart carefully before you start to answer the questions.
- Answer with a single word, or a name, or in figures. If a name is the answer, you can write the full name (e.g. John Smith).
- Check your answers carefully.
- Make sure that you have read and understood any footnotes or asterisks connected to the chart. There are none in this question, but they often appear on other papers.

The model answer for this question is in Appendix 2, page 209.

QUESTION 4: A CHART

Situation: You work in the general office of Designer Decors Ltd, a company which makes ready-made curtains and drapes. The new owner, Mr Tomio Sawada, accompanied by his wife, is due to visit the factory on 4 December. The Personnel Officer tells you about the plans for the visit as follows:

'They'll arrive at 1000 and spend the first hour of the visit having coffee with the MD. Then he'll hand them over to John Snowden for a 2-hour tour of the workshops. John can't be with them for the whole time, so Angela Chiu will take over from him for the second half of the tour. They'll have lunch at 1300 with the MD and with Glenn Clark, the Overseas Sales Director. Lunch will last for an hour. After that they go with the MD to the showroom to open the new display area and talk to customers until 1500. The MD has to leave then for London, so Paul Price, the Workshop Manager, will escort them to the boardroom for the Presentation of Apprentices' Certificates. That starts at 1530. The Area Training Officer, Tony Hart, will be there as well.'

Task: Use the information above to **complete the Visitors' Activity Form below**.

DESIGNER DECORS LTD
VISITORS' ACTIVITY FORM

Name(s) of Visitor(s) _____

Date of Visit _____

STARTING TIME	ACTIVITY	STAFF IN CHARGE	OTHER STAFF OR GUESTS

(20 marks)

Candidates were asked to complete a chart-based timetable detailing the visit to a curtain factory by the new owner and his wife . . . .

This question was well handled by the best candidates, but caused problems for weaker candidates. The information given in the situation required careful reading. Candidates had to produce a timetable of activities for the visit, along with the names of staff who were in charge at particular stages of the visit. The names of the new owner and his wife, Mr and Mrs Tomio Sawada, were too often translated into 'Tomio Sawada and his wife', which would not have shown sufficient respect at the head of the chart. A suitable alternative (and one that was allowed for the full available marks) was 'Mr Tomio Sawada and Mrs Sawada'. Elsewhere in the chart too many candidates put in, not only the name of the member of staff in charge, but also their position in the company, which was unnecessary. The very weak candidates confused the times for the various activities – some even showing Mr Sawada's departure for London before he had completed the final activity!

The model answer for this question is in Appendix 2, page 210.

Appendices

Appendix 1: Answers to selected exercises and questions

Answers to exercises in Chapter 3

Exercise 3.1

1 Peacock and Bryson
52 Railway Road
Bournemouth
BR1 5PW
England

2 Lee's Bicycles
2 Bank Street
Birmingham
BM2 3JD
England

3 Eurodome Rooflights
15 Frinton Street
London
N15 2EL
England

4 Cormack Plumbing Engineers
27 Norval Road
London
N23 2LS
England

5 Martha Fashions Limited
14 Thames Road
London
SW14 3MT
England

6 Jessica Software
35 Chestnut Avenue
London
SW6 2LM
England

Exercise 3.2

1 Ms Ruth Bailey
Managing Director
Stratton Cycles
47 Franklin Avenue
London
SE22 5US
England

Dear Ms Bailey

2 James Elliot
Chief Accountant
Thompson Electrical Goods
19 Woburn Terrace
London
E8 2ML
England

Dear Mr Elliott

3 Andrew Forsythe
Design Department
Victoria Yachts
17 Golders Quay
Bristol
B43 4NW
England

Dear Mr Forsythe

4 Carol Browne
Managing Director
Harvester Enterprises
537 Girton Road
London
N23 45US
England

Dear Ms Browne

5 Mrs Nancy Lorimer
   Editorial Department
   Morden Publishers
   72 Finchley Gardens
   London
   SW11 2RL
   England

   Dear Mrs Lorimer

6 John Burns
   Managing Director
   Alpha Security
   89 Surrey Way
   Cambridge
   CB45 8LK
   England

   Dear Mr Burns

7 Miss Florence Lees
   Chief Buyer
   Link Fashion House
   92 Semple Way
   Oxford
   OX56 7PM
   England

   Dear Miss Lees

8 Desmond Fitzgerald
   Chief Designer
   Saunders Toys
   17 Nicholson Road
   Leeds
   L54 9TR
   England

   Dear Mr Fitzgerald

Exercise 3.6

Situation no	Correct salutation	Correct complimentary close
1	Dear Mr Jenks	Yours sincerely
2	Dear Mr Strauss	Yours sincerely
3	Dear Mrs Vucic	Yours sincerely
4	Dear Sir	Yours faithfully
5	Dear Madam	Yours faithfully
6	Dear Mrs Papas	Yours sincerely
7	Dear Madam	Yours faithfully
8	Dear Mrs Kapaldi	Yours sincerely
9	Dear Sir	Yours faithfully
10	Dear Ms Braun	Yours sincerely

Answers to revision test (Section 3.4) in Chapter 3

Question 1 Addresses

Mrs P Horrocks
654 Somerset Road
Blackburn
BB4 7PD
England

Ms Jelena Pavlovic
Franca Rosamana 16
Novi Sad 4000
Jugoslavia

Mr Jean Aruvée
Henri Charot Wines Ltd
16 Avenue des Abeilles
Belleville
France

Question 2 Salutation and complimentary close

Dear Sir	Yours faithfully
Dear Ms Moore	Yours sincerely
Dear Sir	Yours faithfully
Dear Mr Lee	Yours sincerely
Dear Ms Sidat	Yours sincerely

Question 3 Five missing items

1 Number and street name (for example: 34 Wood Lane)
2 Name of town or city (for example: Birmingham)
3 Number and street name (for example: 145 Tolpuddle Street)
4 Dear Sir
5 Yours faithfully

Question 4 Five mistakes

1 The number and street name should come immediately after 'The Pet Shop'.
2 Date order: 6 January 2001.
3 'kostellanos' should be written 'Kostellanos'.
4 Salutation: 'Dear Ms Kostellanos'.
5 Complimentary close: 'Yours sincerely'.

Question 5 Layout

Top Class Papers Ltd
82 Plaza Gardens
Ho Chi Minh City
Vietnam

Suitable date

The Stock Controller
Foursquare Books Ltd
67 East 55th Street
New York 65307
USA

Dear Sir

Yours faithfully
[Signature]
Assistant Manager

Answers to exercises in Chapter 5

Exercise 5.1

1 FALSE	2 FALSE	3 TRUE	4 FALSE	5 FALSE
6 FALSE	7 FALSE	8 FALSE	9 TRUE	10 FALSE

Exercise 5.2

1 FALSE (b)   2 TRUE (b)   3 TRUE (a)   4 FALSE (a)   5 FALSE (a)

Exercise 5.3

1 False   usually/a day or two later
2 False   a lot of time/an instant
3 False   just once
4 False   reads it/computer
5 False   saver/time and money
6 False   same process (is used)
7 False   single click/mouse OR single stroke/keyboard
8 True   anywhere/in the world
9 True   whole documents/can be sent
10 False   use/more and more

Exercise 5.4

1 True   6% more/each year
2 True   already stored/on computer disks
3 False   makes us use/more paper
4 False   things go wrong/data get lost
5 False   Western Europe alone/30 million
6 True   about/20 years
7 False   everything we buy/packed using paper
8 False   several pages/long
9 False   paper receipts, bills, statements
10 True   Half/people we do not know

Exercise 5.5

1 True   between 1859/and 1869
2 False   Egyptian workers/without machines
3 False   only/by day
4 False   now/very few
5 False   half (of the canal)
6 False   British government/principal shareholder
7 False   French/Egyptian
8 False   safe/and quick
9 True   25,000/20,000
10 False   most ships/carry cargo

Exercise 5.6

1 True   manually/automatically
2 True   depend on/much

3 True   quite common/save time and money

4 True   no matter/where we are

5 True   completely/unnecessary

6 False   travelling by plane/boat

7 False   give number/debit OR credit card

8 False   save a lot/of money

9 True   affected forever/how we communicate

10 False   invented/in 1976

Exercise 5.7

1 False   pet food/paint

2 True   numbers/are declining

3 False   breeding and feeding/controlled conditions

4 False   pollute sea/kill some (fish)

5 True   how many days/how many fish

6 False   12.5/million

7 False   several weeks/at a time

8 False   30%/exporting

9 True   half the people/less than 100 km

10 True   causes hardship/consumers do not buy

Answers to exercises in Chapter 6

Exercise 6.1

1 France

2 2

3 Yes

4 Cotnari

5 No

Exercise 6.2

1 Easter Flowers

2 City Foundation

3 3

4 2

5 2

6 No

7 City Foundation

8 11

9 False

10 Mayor

Exercise 6.3

1 £3.60
2 Thirlspot
3 £7.20
4 £3.60
5 13.00
6 Hourly
7 Yes
8 Preston
9 No
10 60
11 £4.50
12 No
13 £3.60
14 Red Line Transport
15 12
16 Naddle
17 3
18 £7.20
19 4
20 £9.00

Exercise 6.4

1 3
2 Italian Cookery
3 Cooking in Vietnam
4 2
5 P. Laval
6 2
7 No
8 2
9 D. Sung
10 No
11 3
12 $US18.99
13 6
14 Mediterranean Food
15 David
16 Cooking in Vietnam
17 2
18 No
19 4
20 1

Exercise 6.5

1 Axwell
2 2
3 Carvel
4 Yes
5 Sheraton
6 Sangster
7 Yes
8 2
9 Carvel
10 A
11 Fairfax
12 3
13 5
14 Fairfax
15 Yes
16 No
17 7 days
18 4
19 Carvel
20 5

Exercise 6.6

1 Supervisory Management
2 5
3 No
4 Mail Merge 2
5 Business Technology
6 No
7 1
8 2
9 1
10 1
11 Text Processing
12 Practice Management
13 No
14 1
15 Yes
16 No
17 No
18 Yes
19 Business Administration
20 Business Technology

Exercise 6.7

 1 Mercury

 2 5

 3 No

 4 Barbera

 5 1

 6 Corniche

 7 Maipo

 8 Yes

 9 1

10 No

11 1

12 Barbera

13 2

14 Maipo

15 Larnaca

16 4

17 3

18 D

19 $270

20 Benidorm

Answers to exercises in Chapter 7

Exercise 7.1

Stelzer International Staffing Chart

Branch	Year of opening	Name of manager
Oslo	1997	Oskar Gunnarsen
Ho Chi Minh City	1998	Lee Cheng
Toronto	1999	Hannah Samuels
Warsaw	Current year	Brenda Roche or not appointed

Comment

This requires some care in sorting out. First it must be **in order of opening date**. The key date is 1999 – this gives us the means to confirm dates of other openings. The Warsaw office is not yet open, **but will be this year**. The office has no manager appointed, so either of the answers given in the chart is acceptable.

Exercise 7.2

Diary

February	Contact person	Place
Monday 14	Danielle Brisson	New York
Tuesday 15		
Wednesday 16	Hans Kleidermann	Stuttgart Systems
Thursday 17		
Friday 18		
Saturday 19	Cesar Vaccaro	Madrid
Sunday 20		
Monday 21	Barbara Gallo	London
Tuesday 22		
Wednesday 23	Lee Tan	Hanoi
Thursday 24	Lee Tan	Hanoi
Friday 25	Jack Bowen	Phnom Penh
Saturday 26		
Sunday 27		
Monday 28		

Comment

This is a simple exercise; you just need to take your time to read carefully. The only Wednesday for Hans Kleidermann is the 16th. The 'following Monday' is the 21st. Jack Bowen must be on the Friday (the day after Thursday night). The 14th is booked, so Cesar Vaccaro must be met on Saturday the 19th.

Exercise 7.3

1 Rotraut Singspiel
2 Joint MD
3 Personal Assistant
4 Irene Lucic
5 Walter Kort
6 Personnel Director
7 Peter Weiss
8 Nazema Shah
9 Allan Smith
10 Personnel Manager
11 Candidate's name
12 Sam Levene
13 Colin Joseph
14 Sales Assistant (UK)

15 Plant Maintenance Assistant

16 Bernard Brisson

17 Welfare Assistant

18 Angela Mottram

19 Tom Pink

20 Blank or vacancy

Comment

This type of question calls for very careful reading. You have to sort the names and titles skilfully, or you will go wrong. The only reference to the Sales Manager's identity is in the first paragraph of the situation – it is, in fact, *yourself!*

The 4 directors present a tricky problem. You have to remember that Rotraut Singspiel looks after Production and **Personnel**, so 6 and 7 are Personnel Director and Peter Weiss.

The assistants are, perhaps, the most difficult. Production and Plant Maintenance Assistants have the same titles, unlike Sales and Personnel. You also have to note that one assistant in Plant Maintenance has **left the firm**, so this should be made clear by writing 'vacant' or 'left' in box 20.

NEVER LEAVE A BOX COMPLETELY EMPTY. THE EXAMINER CANNOT GIVE YOU A MARK, IF YOU DO THAT. YOU MUST GIVE SOME INDICATION THAT YOU HAVE READ AND UNDERSTOOD.

Exercise 7.4

ARTEMIS CLOTHING COMPANY

Theft Report Form
(COMPLETE IN CAPITALS)

1	Date of incident	**22 January**
2	Time of incident	**22.30**
3	Incident reported by (name and dept)	**Jackie Chan (Security)**
4	Were police informed?	**Yes**
5	Time police arrived	**22.55**
6	Description of intruders	**3 men/1 tall/1 with beard and limp**
7	Was a vehicle involved?	**Yes**
8	Description of vehicle	**Ford van/664DKT**
9	Name(s) of witnesses★	**None**
10	Description of stolen goods	**150 ladies' coats**
		100 men's jackets
11	Estimated value of goods	**£5,000**
12	Report completed by	
	Name	**Candidate's name**
	Department	**Sales and Administration**
	Signature	**Signature of candidate**
	Date	**23 January**

★ other than person named in 3 above

Comment

This is really quite an easy question. You have to be careful with the dates. The theft was **yesterday** and the date for the bottom is **23 January**. You must also take care with the time the police arrived – **15 minutes after the phone call**. Careless reading would make some students write 22.45, which is 15 minutes after the theft took place.

Exercise 7.5

ELITE CARS LTD

Client collection schedule

Name	Time	Flight no	Arriving from	Hotel
Walter Langlauf	10.00	LO5293	Warsaw	Majestic
Helga Weiss	10.10	SK525	Stockholm	Ritz
David Lowe	12.40	BA1605	London	Plaza
Melissa Crane	14.30	AMM1560	Boston	Meridian

Comment

There are 3 points here that call for careful reading. The first is Melissa's change of flight, which makes her arrival time 14.30 **and not 12.30**. The second point is that David Lowe wants to be collected **an hour after he lands**, making his pick up time 12.40. The third point is that you are told to make the list out **in arrival time order**. If you do not note that instruction, you will lose marks.

Exercise 7.6

February

Day	Date	Diary entry
Monday	1	Free
Tuesday	2	Management meeting
Wednesday	3	Group training
Thursday	4	Charity committee
Friday	5	Complete sales report
Saturday	6	
Sunday	7	
Monday	8	Sales assistant interviews
Tuesday	9	Management meeting
Wednesday	10	Lunch – golf club
Thursday	11	Out of office
Friday	12	Out of office
Saturday	13	
Sunday	14	Secretary's birthday
Monday	15	Budget meeting
Tuesday	16	Management meeting

▶

Wednesday	17	Group training
Thursday	18	Free
Friday	19	Free
Saturday	20	
Sunday	21	
Monday	22	Meet Sunila Arshad
Tuesday	23	Management meeting
Wednesday	24	Lunch – golf club
Thursday	25	Charity committee
Friday	26	Free
Saturday	27	
Sunday	28	

Comment

There is a need for careful reading here. There are 2 entries for the 8th, which means that the entry 'Budget meeting' must be put in on the 15th of the month. The 'regular' meetings need to be carefully written into the diary. You have to write 'free' in all no entry days. Many students would miss that. They would also write 'free' in the Saturdays and Sundays, when you are told to leave them blank. If you are told to leave something blank, then do so, **but only if you are told to do it**. Otherwise put in some answer which shows you have understood.

Exercise 7.7

PINES HOTEL AND CONFERENCE CENTRE
Conference booking form
(COMPLETE IN CAPITALS)

Name of company	**DANBY CLARK plc**
Address	**6 LONDON WALL**
	LONDON EC1 5JJ
Telephone	**0171-600-1111**
Title of function	**UK MARKETING AWARDS**
Date of function	**20 July**
Times	From: **12.00 NOON** To: **18.00**
Suite	**PRINCE OF WALES**
Number of persons	**200**
Meals required	**LUNCH** Time: **13.30**
Number of tables	**20**
Other requirements	**1 DRINKS/12.30/CHAMPAGNE/ NON-ALCOHOLIC**
	2 COACH/11.45
	3 LARGE TV SCREEN
	4 VIDEO RECORDER
Invoice to	**MS GAIL KOWALSKI**

Comment

The main difficulty in this question is the times. You have to be careful. The room is needed from 12.00 noon, but the event does not actually start until 12.30. Lunch is an hour **after that at 13.30**. Lunch must be over by **15.00**. This leads to the end of the awards (2 hours) at **17.00**. The letter asks for another hour to 'be on the safe side'. The final time, therefore, **must be recorded as 18.00**.

The letter also asks for tables for 10 persons, so the **number of tables is 20**.

Some candidates would lose marks by not being careful to record the other requirements accurately.

Answers to exercises in Chapter 8

Exercise 8.1

1 The customer (telephones) our office.

2 The photocopier usually (works) very well.

3 The interview (takes) place at 11 o'clock today.

4 How (is) he today?

5 They (have) an appointment with the MD. They (hope) to complete the contract.

6 We (send) out invoices on Mondays.

7 On most days she (assists) her supervisor.

8 They (offer) a discount for cash when we (buy) in bulk.

9 He (arrives) soon. His flight (is) late.

10 (Have) you a pen, please? I (wish) to write a note.

Exercise 8.2

1 I (am arriving) at 11 o'clock and I (am bringing) the contract with me.

2 She (is asking) for permission to leave early; she (is meeting) her son.

3 You (are having) difficulty with the fax machine. It (is working) badly.

4 They (are walking) to the hotel and they (are having) lunch there.

5 He (is writing) a letter to the delivery agent. He (is complaining) about the delay.

6 We (are waiting) for the taxi. It (is taking) us to the airport.

7 The bus (is waiting) outside. The driver (is reading) the newspaper.

8 The documents (are coming) by special courier before noon.

9 Some of the staff (are losing) their jobs tomorrow. They (are protesting) to the MD. He (is trying) to find them jobs in another company.

10 We (are holding) a competition today. All the staff (are entering). The MD (is giving) a prize for the best entry. The winner (is going) on a holiday to Italy.

Exercise 8.3

1 He (clapped) his hands when he (heard) the result.

2 The planes (landed) at 2-minute intervals.

3 The office lift (stopped) working at noon yesterday. It (started) again at teatime.

4 I (booked) the tickets last week. I (made) the hotel reservation at the same time.

5 She (complained) about the noise. I (told) her to ignore it.

6 Yesterday we (interviewed) for a secretary. We (decided) not to appoint anyone.

7 The firm (advertised) its latest products on TV. We (showed) the advertisement 6 times.

8 The parcel (weighed) 20 kilos. The post office (refused) to handle it for us.

9 Our new MD (visited) the factory yesterday. She (brought) her daughter with her.

10 You (thought) the order was for 1,000 boxes. The customer's letter (stated) that he only (wanted) 100 boxes. You (despatched) too many boxes.

Exercise 8.4

1 We (have written) to the Chairman and he (has sent) his reply.

2 The accountant (has shown) that our profits (have fallen).

3 She (has arrived) by taxi. I (have paid) the driver.

4 When you (have finished) your typing you can go. I (have completed) the other jobs.

5 We (have invited) a number of customers. So far, seven (have accepted) our invitation.

6 He (has refused) our offer. He (has taken) his business to another firm.

7 We (have established) our new delivery system. The transport manager (has trained) all the delivery drivers.

8 She (has repaired) the photocopier, and she (has left) a new instruction manual.

9 Our staff magazine (has introduced) a new feature about hobbies. Six members of staff (have contributed) to the first article.

10 Our department (has purchased) new desks and chairs for all staff. The supplier (has taken) all the old furniture.

Exercise 8.5

1 We (are coming) to your office (tomorrow).

2 The delivery van (is arriving) at 10 o'clock in the (morning).

3 The team (is working) throughout the (day).

4 I (am asking) for permission to visit the factory (soon).

5 The complaints procedure (is starting) (next) month.

6 Six new employees (are beginning) work for us (today).

7 We (are preparing) the conference room (immediately).

8 The wages department (is preparing) your wage slip (tomorrow).

9 All members of staff (are going) to the celebration (next Tuesday).

10 You (are finishing) your employment with us (in one hour).

Exercise 8.6

1 I (shall go) to their offices tomorrow.

2 The flight (will take) 5 hours.

3 They (will order) the meal shortly.

4 She (will buy) a new computer.

5 You (will receive) new instructions by e-mail.

6 We (shall try) to satisfy your request.

7 You and my secretary (will meet) to arrange the conference.

8 The supplier (will give) us a discount.

9 Many employees (will take) their holidays in June.

10 The parts (will arrive) by road.

Exercise 8.7

1 I am going to go to their offices tomorrow.
2 The flight is going to take 5 hours.
3 They are going to order the meal shortly.
4 She is going to buy a new computer.
5 You are going to receive new instructions by e-mail.
6 We are going to try to satisfy your request.
7 You and my secretary are going to meet to arrange the conference.
8 The supplier is going to give us a discount.
9 Many employees are going to take their holidays in June.
10 The parts are going to arrive by road.

Exercise 8.8

1 Please bring the documents to my office now.
2 In order to avoid breaking it, carry the parcel with care.
3 Please count the number of visitors at the meeting.
4 Please visit the despatch department today.
5 Please place the article on my desk before noon.
6 Write the invitations by hand.
7 Please order the replacement machine as soon as possible.
8 Please tell the workforce they have earned a bonus this month.
9 Please go to the supervisor and apologise for your mistake.
10 Please remember to close the door; make sure the door is locked.

Exercise 8.9

1 If you took out a contract, we (would) certainly offer a discount.
2 You (must) finish your work before you leave the office.
3 If you are not sure, you (can) always ask for advice.
4 It is not certain, but we (may) ask for a reference.
5 If he did not come by air, then he (would) probably come by train.
6 If he does not come by train, he (will) probably catch a plane.
7 You (can) call me on my mobile 24 hours a day.
8 You (may) be right, but it is difficult to decide at the moment.
9 The deadline is 3 o'clock, so we (must) reach a decision now.
10 I (will) ensure personally that all the parts are delivered.
11 In ordinary circumstances that (would) do very well.
12 (May) I take the documents now, please?
13 (Must) you leave so early? It is only 2 o'clock.
14 If you had a problem with the copier, we (would) send someone at once.
15 If you have a problem, we (will) send someone at once.
16 She has no choice in the matter; she (must) sign the contract today.
17 Why (must) you go? It is a meeting for assistants.

18 If your service does not improve, we (may) decide to go to another firm.

19 We are 100% reliable and therefore we (can) guarantee total satisfaction.

20 They (may) vote to strike, so I (must) go there at once.

Exercise 8.10

1 If you want (my) opinion, just ask me.

2 Has he completed all (his) work for the day?

3 She will soon realise that (her) new job is very demanding.

4 Have Tom and Anna left? (Their) cars are still in the car park.

5 If you give me (their) address, I will write to them.

6 Is (my) hair untidy? I want to make a good impression.

7 I cannot contact Mrs Petrangeli. (Her) mobile phone must be switched off.

8 Please accept (our) congratulations. We think (your) new book is very good.

9 Please tell Jane that (her) appointment with him is for 2 o'clock.

10 Did Anna write this letter? Why must I correct (her) mistakes?

11 I went to Johnson's Ltd yesterday and ate in (their) executive dining room.

12 The owner, Carlo Trevino, says that (his/their) ideas are up to date, but a lot of (his/their) equipment is too old.

13 If you need to write to Janet and James, I will give you (their) addresses before I leave.

14 We have spoken to (our) own lawyers about the matter. That is what we pay them for.

15 Where is Ravi Arshad? He has not finished (his) report.

16 Please help us and ask the theatre to change (our) tickets; we are going to be late.

17 You cannot help her. (Her) decision to leave is her own.

18 I want them to know that (my) car is at (their) disposal.

19 She always carries (her) handbag on (her) left shoulder.

20 Unlike John I like to take (my) time. (His) method is to rush into things.

Exercise 8.11

1 (This) book here is a very good guide.

2 I like (those) computer games over there.

3 Which desk would you like? (This) one here, or the one over there?

4 (These) tools I have here are very useful.

5 Does (this) road we are on take us to Rome?

6 I have told you before about Quickfast. (That) firm is not reliable.

7 May I show you (those) documents I mentioned yesterday?

8 Which of you has written (that) report over there on my desk?

9 I do not like (this) airport. It is always as busy as this.

10 She says she will send (those) files you asked for at once.

11 I do not like (those) suggestions you made yesterday. I prefer (these) ideas that Hannah has just given to me.

12 (This) dress I am wearing is most suitable.

13 (Those) shoes you showed me last night will match (that) dress I wore on Friday.

14 Do not lose (those) plans I gave you.

15 Some of (those) staff we met yesterday are very clever.

16 (These) parcels here are for immediate despatch, but (those) crates in the corner can go tomorrow.

17 (Those) decisions we took yesterday are final. We cannot keep having (these) uncertainties.

18 If you will take (those) people over there, I will look after (these) people here.

19 (These) drawings in my hand are for the new factory.

20 (That) word processor next door is very old. Replace it with one of (those) word processors we bought yesterday.

Exercise 8.12

1 Last month's sales figures were very (good), but this month's are even (better).

2 He is the (best) worker in this department, but Ann Park over in Sales is even (better).

3 The attitude of our staff is very (good); in fact, it could not be (better).

4 This is without doubt the (best) photocopier on the market.

5 We make many (good) products, but on a few occasions we make something that is (better).

6 There is (some) paper on the desk, and there is (more) in the drawer.

7 There are (more) people in the USA than in Norway.

8 I wish to buy (some) books, please. Do you have any (more) downstairs?

9 Of all the people I work with, I like Tina the (most).

10 The (more) I see her, the (more) I like her style.

11 I have brought you a (little) present.

12 There is (less) paper in the stockroom than I thought there was.

13 It is the (least) I can do to say thank you.

14 Most employees are paid (less) than yourself.

15 Of all the jobs we have to do, this is the (least) important.

Exercise 8.13

1 It is very hot in the office today. Shall we go (outside) for a while?

2 I'm getting cold out here. Shall we go back (inside) the building?

3 (Everywhere) you look, you can see people working.

4 I have looked (everywhere) for that file, but I cannot find it.

5 There are no restrictions; you can go (anywhere) you like in the building.

6 Did you come (here) on the train?

7 I followed instructions and went (there) by the shortest route.

8 When we stood (here/inside) in the entrance hall, we saw no-one, but as soon as we went (there/outside), there were people (everywhere) you looked.

9 He is a real globe-trotter. He travels (everywhere) in the world. He will go (anywhere) you want him to go.

10 I have looked (everywhere) for Tom, but I cannot find him (anywhere). Do you think he came (here) first or went straight (there)?

Exercise 8.14

1 This calculator is (mine); (yours) is on the desk, Jane.

2 John bought the pen, so it must be (his), even though Anna says it is (hers).

3 Both Ali and Petra did the work, so the responsibility is (theirs).

4 You are late for lunch. We have already eaten (ours), but (yours) has gone cold.

5 We have done nothing wrong. The mistake must be (yours), Janet.

6 The decision we make is (ours); the decision the rest make is (theirs).

7 Why can Lucia and Paolo never agree if something is (hers) or (his)?

8 I don't like my calculator, Hannah. Can I please borrow (yours)?

9 The assistant managers are angry. The managers have BMWs, but (theirs) are only Volvos.

10 Since this letter is addressed to me, it must be (mine).

11 I have just seen my new office, Helga. Have you seen (yours) yet?

12 Rozi says she is sure the bag is (yours). She saw you buy it last week.

13 Salma and Anisha have a really nice office. I envy them. I really prefer (theirs) to (mine).

14 We have booked tickets on the 3 o'clock train. Do you think that train on platform 2 will be (ours)?

15 I am happy with my working hours, Andy, but you are lucky, because (yours) are more convenient than mine.

16 Bob and Rupert will have to leave their office; it is (theirs) that I want.

17 Barbara lost a bag like that last week. I am sure it is (hers).

18 The MD has just given me my new car. He says he will give you (yours) tomorrow.

19 If you want the job, then it is (yours).

20 The sales team have worked hard to win the contract. The success is (theirs) alone.

Exercise 8.15

1 There is (nothing) I want you to do for me.

2 (Everyone) sincerely hopes that the meeting is a success.

3 Is there (anyone/someone) who can tell me what to do?

4 It is ridiculous. I have asked (everyone/everybody) in the office and (no-one/nobody) knows how to send an e-mail.

5 I have all the information. There is (nothing) more that I need.

6 There is (something) wrong with the delivery system. (Everybody/Everyone) on our list is complaining.

7 Is (anyone) doing (anything) about this broken fax machine?

8 This fax machine has been broken for 3 weeks. Will (someone) please do (something) about it?

9 (No-one/nobody) must enter my room without knocking.

10 (Someone) has taken the safe key and not returned it. Does (anyone) know (anything) about it?

11 I want to see (everyone) in my office now. (No-one/nobody) must ignore this request. I have (something) important to tell you all.

12 If you have worked for 5 years, you receive a bonus. This applies to (everyone/everybody).

13 Could (someone/somebody) please close that door?

14 I hope that (everything) is to your satisfaction.

15 It seems to be well planned. I cannot think of (anything) else that needs doing or (anyone) else to write to.

16 This is our secret. You must tell (no-one/nobody) else.

17 I cannot keep the secret. I must tell (someone) else.

18 I have told you (everything) I know about it.

19 The MD shook hands with (everyone/everybody) and congratulated them.

20 (Everyone/everybody) must work hard this week. There is (someone/somebody) coming to inspect the firm. The MD wants (nothing) to go wrong. (Everything) depends on making a good impression.

Exercise 8.16

1 I think I have covered everything, but please ring me (if) you have further questions.

2 He told me (that) he would find a solution to the problem.

3 We cannot attend the meeting, (because) our MD is on holiday.

4 Do you know (where) you are going after you leave Seattle?

5 (When) I receive your order, I shall despatch it at once.

6 It is very important (that) we all agree on the matter.

7 (Because) plans are not yet complete, I cannot tell you any more.

8 Did he say (where) he was taking the drawings to?

9 The hotel will be booked, (if/when) there is enough money.

10 (If) you do not do as we ask, we cannot make the payment.

11 She was sacked, (because) she refused to work overtime.

12 You must wait in the hall, (until) you are sent for.

13 You must go to the canteen, (where) the visitors are waiting for you.

14 (If) you wish to place an order, please telephone us today.

15 He could not leave the hotel, (until) the fax came through.

16 He has not told us, (when) he will be arriving.

17 She will do the extra work, (if) I ask her nicely.

18 It is for these reasons (that) we must increase production.

19 John will not come to work today, (because) he has a cold.

20 Shall we go somewhere quiet, (where) we can discuss the matter?

Exercise 8.17

1 Scotland is situated to the (north) of England.

2 Mexico is situated to the (south) of the USA.

3 The sun always sets in the (west).

4 Europeans describe Japan as part of the Far (East).

5 The office is very (close/near) to the airport.

6 How (far) is it to your office? A few miles?

7 Take the first turning on the (left), then go (straight) ahead for 100 metres.

8 Remember to turn (right), not left at the bank.

9 Tuesday is the day after (Monday).

10 At the (weekend) we usually go to the beach.

11 The day after (Tuesday) is Wednesday.

12 Can you please tell me the (time)? Is it 3 o'clock yet?

13 He will be arriving at 6 o'(clock).

14 How many (minutes) are there in an hour? There are 60.

15 In a race every (second) counts.

16 I will not repeat myself. I shall say this only (once).

17 The machine broke down on Monday and on Friday. It has broken down (twice).

18 The race (starts) at 2 o'clock. It (ends/finishes) at 4 o'clock.

19 What was the winner's (finishing) time? It was under 2 hours.

20 You must (promise/try) to keep this a secret.

Exercise 8.18

1 How (long) is this road? 2 kilometers.

2 Is this shelf (wide) enough for those files?

3 How much does the fax machine (weigh)? About 22 kilos.

4 Don't worry. It's only a (small) problem.

5 The Eiffel Tower in Paris is a very (tall) building.

6 In a very (short) time he will be promoted.

7 How (heavy) is this bicycle? Does it (weigh) more than 10 kilos?

8 Can you stretch your arms out (wide)?

9 Your desk is 2 meters long; mine is 1.5 meters long. Mine is (shorter) than yours.

10 I do not wish to keep you, so my speech will be quite (short).

11 These envelopes are quite (expensive). They cost 50 cents each.

12 Our policy is to buy (cheap) machines and replace them often.

13 The job is not an (easy) one. It calls for hard work.

14 Because of his strong views, he is a (difficult) person to work with.

15 Thanking people is good, but praising them is (better).

16 The July sales figures are bad, but the figures for June are even (worse).

17 All you have to do is sign it. It is not a (difficult) task.

18 These envelopes are (cheap). I expected them to be much more.

19 He should like his watch. It was quite (expensive).

20 Now that we have the loan, I am sure things will get (better).

Exercise 8.19

Afternoon in the office

Dieter:
Good (afternoon), Janet. Can I (introduce) you to Mrs Palmieri, our new Sales (Manager/Director)? I have (invited) her to look round the production (department).

Janet:
Good (afternoon), Mrs Palmieri. I am very (pleased) to meet you. We have (heard) a lot about you. I look (forward) very much to (working) with you.

Mrs Palmieri:
It's a great (pleasure) to meet you, Janet. Please (call) me Anna. I am sure I shall (enjoy) working with you all. Will you be (attending) the meeting later this (afternoon)?

Janet:
No, I'm afraid I must give my (apologies). I have to (leave) in an hour. I am catching a (plane) to New York. I hope my secretary has (booked) my seat. Dieter, before I (go), will you take care of Saturday's (conference) at the Plaza (Hotel) in Brighton? Make sure you (introduce) yourself to Farida Shah. She is the hotel (manager) and she promised to give us the very (best) conference room. Well, I (must) be on my (way). I have some (letters) to write before I (leave).

Dieter:
Don't worry, Janet. I'll (take) care of everything at the (conference/Plaza). Now, Anna, I'll give you a quick (tour) of the (production) department.

Mrs Palmieri:
(Thank) you very (much), Dieter. And thank you, (Janet). Have a good (time) in New York. I (wish) I was (going) myself. It's a very exciting (city/place). I have a daughter who (works/lives) in Washington. Perhaps we can have a (chat/talk) about it when you (return). Right, Dieter, lead on. You are my (guide) for the next half (hour).

Exercise 8.20

At the conference

Davina Kaur is talking to Paul Levkas.

Davina:
Hello, Paul. I was (hoping) you would be at the (conference). Do you (remember) me? We met a few days (ago) at the music (concert/festival).

Paul:
Of course, I (remember) you (very) well indeed. You made the (presentation) to the conductor on (behalf) of your firm. Your short (speech) was very entertaining. How (are) you today?

Davina:
I'm very (well), thank you. You look very well (yourself). I'm so (pleased/glad) that we have (met) again. I (want) to ask your (advice) about a very (important) matter.

Paul:
If I (can) be of some (help), please tell me (about) it.

Davina:
Well, you (know) I work for Sissioni Perfumes. In fact, I've just been (offered) the position of Marketing (Manager/Director). But the truth is, I don't (want) to work for them any (more). I'm not happy with the (methods) they use. They are old fashioned and I would also (prefer) a job with less travelling. I have two sons and a (daughter) and I want to spend more (time) with (them). So what I really (want) is to set up my own (business). Can you give me some (advice) on how to (do) that?

Paul:
Yes, I (can). I had my (own) business for a (number) of years before I took the (job) here. It (might) be better if we arranged an (appointment) at my office. Or I (could) meet you for lunch or (dinner) one evening. I can give you the (names) of some useful (people/contacts). What about (next) Wednesday?

Davina:
I'm (sorry), Paul, I was watching that man over (there). Can you (repeat) what you just said, please?

Paul:
I was (saying) we (could) meet next Wednesday.

Davina:
That's a (good/splendid) idea. (Here/This) is my mobile number. Please (give) me a call soon. I shall (look) forward to (hearing) from you. Goodbye for (now).

Exercise 8.21

1 Can you say that again, please?
2 I am looking forward to your early reply.
3 I would rather not travel to the hotel by taxi.
4 What does he want me to do about the problem?
5 That was a very pleasant lunch we had yesterday.
6 Can you tell us when they will deliver the goods?
7 I am inviting a number of colleagues to the production department.
8 She was very sorry that she missed her appointment.
9 We hope we can be of further help very soon.
10 It has been a pleasure teaching you all these skills.

Appendix 2: Model answers to past examination questions

Model answers to Series 3 1999 questions

QUESTION 1

MEMORANDUM	
TO	All Company Staff
FROM	A N Other i/c Stationery
DATE	As appropriate
SUBJECT	Rising Stationery Costs

The Accounts Manager has written to me to complain about the increasing amount of
stationery being used by company staff in all departments. The cost of these items –
paper, envelopes, notepads, pens, pencils etc – is extremely high, and the Accounts
Manager thinks that there may be a lot of waste.
As the staff member directly responsible for stationery supplies and distribution, I ask
for your full co-operation in making sure that, from now on, you observe the following
practice:
1   Order only the amounts of stationery that you need
2   Check your existing stock on a weekly basis
3   Monitor the total amount being used in your department.
I must stress that it is vital to take note of the Accounts Manager's comments, and to
take action in the interests of the company.
I shall shortly be issuing new guidelines on stationery ordering, and expect to consult
with department heads to decide on best practice for the future. For the moment,
please follow these simple rules and try to cut down the amounts used.

QUESTION 2

1	FALSE	within the reach/of all people
2	FALSE	after 5/claim-free years
3	FALSE	in-patient/costs
4	TRUE	established the longest
5	FALSE	ahead/of all
6	FALSE	fast/choose your doctor
7	TRUE	visiting hours/more flexible OR more convenient
8	FALSE	worldwide/cover OR cover/overseas
9	TRUE	very best/most popular
10	FALSE	Healthline/Information Service

QUESTION 3

1 3
2 Warehouse
3 Hart
4 Norma Wood
5 No
6 1996
7 4
8 No
9 Anna Socic
10 1998
11 3
12 May Wilson
13 Clerical
14 Warehouse
15 1997
16 3
17 8
18 Norma Wood
19 4
20 1995

QUESTION 4

SUNCARE LTD STAFFING ORGANISATION

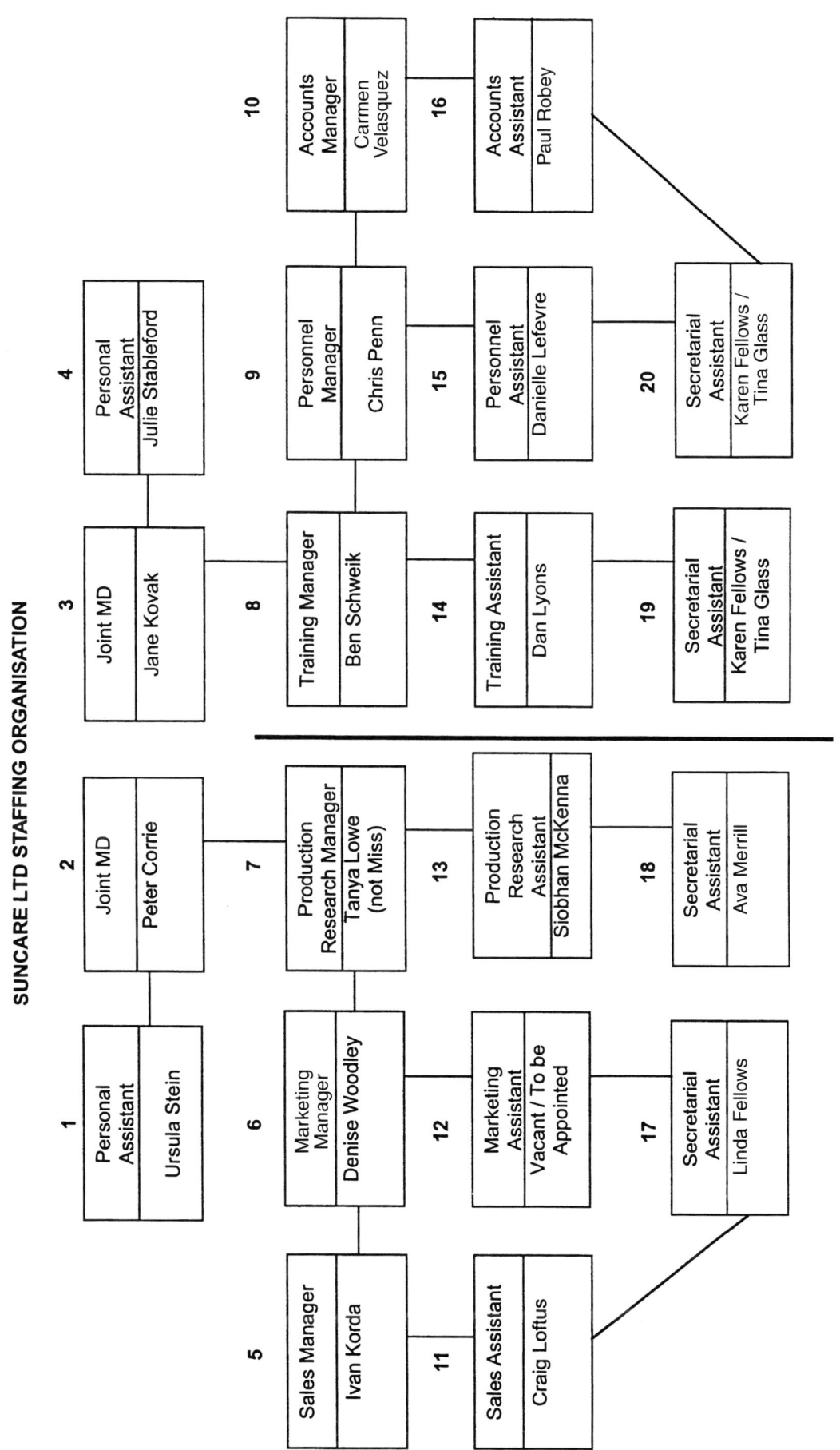

1 Personal Assistant — Ursula Stein

2 Joint MD — Peter Corrie

3 Joint MD — Jane Kovak

4 Personal Assistant — Julie Stableford

5 Sales Manager — Ivan Korda

6 Marketing Manager — Denise Woodley

7 Production Research Manager — Tanya Lowe (not Miss)

8 Training Manager — Ben Schweik

9 Personnel Manager — Chris Penn

10 Accounts Manager — Carmen Velasquez

11 Sales Assistant — Craig Loftus

12 Marketing Assistant — Vacant / To be Appointed

13 Production Research Assistant — Siobhan McKenna

14 Training Assistant — Dan Lyons

15 Personnel Assistant — Danielle Lefevre

16 Accounts Assistant — Paul Robey

17 Secretarial Assistant — Linda Fellows

18 Secretarial Assistant — Ava Merrill

19 Secretarial Assistant — Karen Fellows / Tina Glass

20 Secretarial Assistant — Karen Fellows / Tina Glass

Model answers to Series 4 1999 questions

QUESTION 1

Acme Vacuum Cleaner Company
Fall Birch Road
Henbury
Gloucester
GL2 5ER

9 November 1999

Ms Janet Duxbury
District Education Officer
Atlas House
The Wellsprings
Henbury
Gloucester
GL1 3LD

Dear Ms Duxbury

I am writing to ask permission for our company to use the car park at the James North High School for a 2-week period starting on 22 December.

The reason for this request is that our own car park is due to be resurfaced and redesigned.

The work will take 2 weeks to complete, and we need a suitable car park nearby which can take a hundred cars. The school car park, which is across the road from our factory, would be perfect.

I understand that the school is on holiday during the period we need it whilst the work is being done.

I have spoken to the Head of the school, Mrs Anne Legge, who says she is happy to help. You may know that our company employs several James North pupils every year when they leave the school. Mrs Legge did ask me to contact you, however, for official permission to use the school's car park.

I hope you will be able to give your permission, and I look forward to hearing from you.

Yours sincerely

Candidate's name

QUESTION 2

1	FALSE	another telephone receptionist/extra sales staff
2	TRUE	make/more effective
3	FALSE	no extra/cost
4	FALSE	design/printing
5	FALSE	5,000/until 20 December 1999
6	FALSE	150/throughout UK
7	FALSE	over 21/highly trained
8	FALSE	established/15 years
9	TRUE	7 days/a week
10	TRUE	48 hour/service

QUESTION 3

1	11
2	7
3	5
4	North West
5	North East
6	No
7	Yes
8	3
9	3
10	2
11	No
12	Scotland
13	Newcastle
14	Scotland
15	Wales
16	London
17	South West
18	5
19	7
20	Yes

Appendix 2

QUESTION 4

DESIGNER DECORS LTD
VISITORS' ACTIVITY FORM

Name(s) of Visitor(s) _____ Mr and Mrs Tomio Sawada _____

Date of Visit _____ 4 December _____

STARTING TIME	ACTIVITY	STAFF IN CHARGE	OTHER STAFF OR GUESTS
1000	Meet MD and Coffee	MD	
1100	Workshop tour	J Snowden	
1200	Workshop tour	A Chiu	
1300	Lunch	MD	Glenn Clark
1400	Open Display Area	MD	
1530	Presentation of Apprentice Certificates	Paul Price	Tony Hart

Appendix 3: Advice for students taking the **LCCIEB** First Level English for Business examination

Introduction

Candidates who pass examinations do so for good reasons. They have worked hard to master the syllabus, they have analysed typical questions and model answers from past papers, and through constant practice they have reached a stage where they feel confident to handle whatever the particular examination throws at them. There are no surprises for them and, in the examination, they work to a planned and practised routine that ensures success.

Candidates who fail do so for various reasons. They may be poorly prepared, they may not have covered the whole syllabus, or they may lack vital skills. Most failures however are the result of poor handling in the examination room of the skills they have acquired; they have no planned routine, which helps to keep them on track and able to deal systematically with the paper before them. Basic errors, rushing at a question, failing to read the rubric, and running out of time are the most common faults.

This is where the 'auto-pilot' method comes into its own. It prepares you fully for everything about the examination. You will have memorised the procedure to follow, so that in the examination room you will have a planned routine from the moment that you take your seat, or even before that moment.

The most important thing to remember is – **the Examiner is on your side**. LCCIEB is a positive examination board and its policy is to reward candidates when that is possible. The Examiner is not trying to trip you up. On the contrary, the Examiner is there to make sure you receive what you deserve. Remember that – it can boost your confidence when things get a little tough.

Planning your time

You can plan your time before you enter the examination room. You know how long the exam lasts and you know how many questions there will be. You know that in English for Business First Level you must answer all 4 questions. You also know how many marks there are for each question; this allows you to divide your time accurately. Just to recall the facts for you:

- The examination lasts for 2 hours
- There are 4 questions
- All questions must be answered
- The total marks for the paper are 100
- Questions 1 and 2 are worth 30 marks each
- Questions 3 and 4 are worth 20 marks each.

Because there is no 'reading time' before starting, you must allow 10 minutes to read through the paper. You must also allow 10 minutes to check your answers at the end. This actually leaves you with 1 hour and 40 minutes to deal with the 4 questions. Keep an eye on the clock! You should aim to spend 30 minutes each on Questions 1 and 2, and 20 minutes each on Questions 3 and 4. These timings are not 'rigid', but you need to keep them in mind. If you over-run by a minute or two, there is no problem, but do not over-run by 5 minutes or more; stop answering that question and go on to the next one. You will probably find time at the end to finish the one you left. What you must not do is put yourself in a position where a whole question is rushed or not answered at all. Keep an eye on the clock, and stick to your planned routine at all times.

Final preparations

On the day of the examination, give yourself plenty of time. Make sure your materials are ready. Arrive at the examination centre in good time. Keep calm, and help your colleagues to keep calm. Run through your planned procedure in your mind. If you can, find out before the examination where you will be sitting. Remember that the examination is not a test – **it is an opportunity for you to show your skills**.

When you enter the examination room, stay calm. Find your seat. Lay out your materials. Remember that you have practised everything before many times. You know the questions – only the content is different. And you have the skills to deal with them. Once you start, follow your routine. Read through the paper. Keep to your times for each question. Check your work thoroughly. And never, never leave the examination room before the end of the time. Even if you finish checking, and you still have 10 minutes to go, use the time to re-check your work.

If you do all this, and you have worked hard to develop your skills by following this book, you will pass with flying colours. We wish you 'Good luck', but in truth luck will not be a factor. You will have passed because of your skills, and nothing else!

Index